.R65
1991

# Violent Crime and Gun Control

Gerald D. Robin
*University of New Haven*

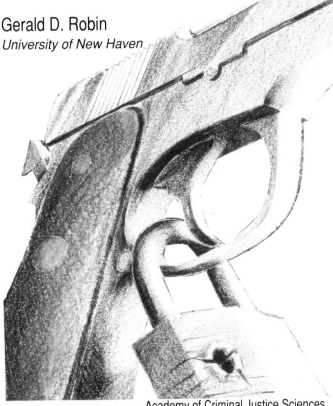

Academy of Criminal Justice Sciences
Northern Kentucky University
402 Nunn Hall
Highland Heights, KY 41076

Anderson Publishing Co.
Criminal Justice Division
P.O. Box 1576
Cincinnati, OH 45201-1576

# Violent Crime and Gun Control

**ISBN** 0-87084-747-3

**Library of Congress Catalog Number** 91-70555

---

Kelly Humble *Managing Editor*                    *Project Editor* Gail Eccleston

Cover Design by John H. Walker

*To my father, Jack Robin, the greatest man I know.*
   *To my loving and wise mother, Sylvia.*
*To the best brother in the world, Gary Robin,*
   *with whom I am forever and inextricably bonded,*
*And to Leonard Stein, my true mentor,*
   *whose guiding hand is with me in every word I write.*

# Acknowledgments

I am indebted to the University of New Haven for awarding me a Research Assistantship during the period that this monograph was being researched and prepared. Without the University's generosity, the completion of this work would have been even more time-consuming and demanding. I also want to thank my research assistant, Gary Schreter, for his outstanding efforts and commitment to this monograph.

—Gerald D. Robin

# Contents

# 1

# The Gun Problem

Were it not for the gun problem in America, there would be no call for or controversy over "gun control." Each year, firearms are involved in about 10,000 murders, 15,000 suicides and almost 2,000 accidental deaths (Baker et al., 1980:224; Wright, 1988:28; Buchalter, 1988:7). Many more people, of course, sustain non-fatal firearm injuries, bringing the total number of firearm-abuse incidents to about one million per year (Wright, 1988:28). From the time President Kennedy was assassinated in November 1963 until November 1982 when President Reagan barely escaped being assassinated, firearms have claimed the lives of over 900,000 Americans—more than the total number of soldiers killed (747,000) in all wars from the Civil War through the Vietnam War (Anderson, 1986:233).

## FIREARMS AND VIOLENT CRIME

As used in this monograph, the gun problem refers specifically to the prominent role played by and relevance of guns in the commission of violent crime and to the social consequences of gun crime. Between 1975 and 1985, three million people were assaulted, robbed or killed with guns (*Newsweek*, 1988a). Firearms are used in:

- between 60 percent and two-thirds of the criminal homicides (*Report to the Nation on Crime and Justice*, 1988:20; Cook, 1983:53).

- 10 percent of rapes.

- almost one-quarter (23%) of the aggravated assaults.

- 41 percent of all (UCR) robberies reported to police, compared with 20 percent of robbery victimizations in the National Crime Survey (Rand et al., 1986:2).[1]

Based on UCR data, the average annual number of crimes committed with guns for the 1974-1983 period was 332,809. Victimization data indicate that, over the 1973-1982 period, the average annual number of gun crimes was 837,278 (see Table 1.1). Although offenders armed with guns actually shot their victims in just 3.5 percent of all violent crimes, they attempted to do so in 21 percent of such victimizations. Over half (58%) of the armed victimizations involved only the threat posed by the presence, display or brandishing of the weapon itself—whose contribution to the fear of crime and of one's personal safety is incalculable (Rand et al., 1986:3-4; Wright, 1986:1). There are no reliable figures on the number of victims who sustain non-fatal injuries from gun crimes, but some estimates place the figure as high as 100,000 to 200,000 per year (USA Today, 1988d).

**Table 1.1 Gun Crime***

| UCR crimes involving any firearms (yearly average 1974-1983) | | NCS victimizations involving guns (yearly average 1973-1982) |
|---|---|---|
| Rape | 17,380† | 17,380 |
| Robbery | 184,992 | 244,960 |
| Aggressive Assault | 120,437 | 564,938 |
| Homicide | 10,000 | 10,000†† |
| | 332,809 | 837,278 |

* Yearly averages are calculated from basic data presented in Tables 1.2, 1.3 and 1.4 (Rand et al., 1986) and in the 1988 Uniform Crime Reports.
† The rape figure is from the National Crime Survey because the UCR does not categorize this offense by whether weapon was present.
††The homicide figure is from the UCR because information on this offense is not collected in the NCS.

*Criminogenic features of firearms.* It is the intrinsic characteristics of firearms which make them so attractive to criminals and more lethal than other readily available likely substitute weapons. Guns pose a credible threat even in the hands of weak, relatively unskilled assailants. They can be used to maim or kill quickly and without sustained effort, in an "impersonal" fashion and from a safe distance. The mere display of a gun will usually immobilize the victim, thwart any attempt to resist or counterattack, and will maximize the offender's chances of success (Cook, 1983:49:55-56). The National Crime Survey found that gun possession is associated with higher crime completion rates than when other weapons are used or the offender is unarmed, e.g., 49 percent of the rapes at gunpoint were completed compared to only 20 percent of those involving knives (Rand et al., 1986:3). Guns are especially effective against the more invulnerable targets such as banks and commercial establishments. These targets are able to be defended against less dangerous weapons; because of this, guns facilitate commercial robberies and lethal assaults on otherwise relatively crime-proof victims (Cook, 1983:49). The choice to use a gun in perpetrating crime may, in itself, signal the criminal's *intention* to harm the victim and enables one to easily convert intention into action; even if there is no *a priori* intent to inflict injury, the outcome may be much the same (Lester, 1984:5-6). Zimring (1968:724,728) found that gun attacks are five times more likely to result in death than assaults with knives; and unlike guns, knives are seldom involved in accidental killings. Gun robberies are 3-4 times more lethal than are other kinds of robbery (National Institute of Justice Crime File).

*Weapons effect.* A series of experiments by Berkowitz (1986:19) and other social psychologists (see Box 1.1) indicates that the mere presence of a weapon can sometimes induce people to become violent, i.e., the presence of a weapon has the effect of "causing" assaultive acts that would not otherwise have occurred. This phenomenon is referred to as the "weapons effect." In our society, guns function as a powerful conditioned stimulus which elicit antisocial behavior by the repeated pairing of guns and rewarded aggression, i.e., the images projected and lesson learned is that aggression "pays off." This relationship is constantly reinforced through the mass media and by personal experience, observation and recollection (Berkowitz, 1981:11). It is this unique quality of guns to control us ("to pull out aggressive reactions") to which Berkowitz (1968:22) refers when he states that "the finger pulls the trigger, but the trigger may also be pulling the finger." The weapons effect is most applicable to persons who are angry, emotionally upset or frustrated and thus predisposed but not wedded toward aggression, such as would occur in domestic arguments or barroom altercations that get out of hand. Since much violence is impulsive rather than planned or intentional, whether the situation culminates in an assault often depends on whether there is an immediate stimulus available (like a gun) to trigger the action (Berkowitz, 1968:19). The weapons effect is one of the major assumptions behind gun control and maintains that widespread firearms availability contributes to violent crime.

*Handguns.* Handguns are at the core of the gun problem, violent crime and contemporary gun control efforts (Drinan, 1976:52). Although handguns make up only about one-fourth of all privately owned firearms, they account for a disproportionate amount of the violent crime, e.g., close to 50 percent of all murders (NBC Summer Showcase, 1988:30; Gettinger, 1980:9; Kaplan, 1981:19). An especially tragic dimension to the profile of handgun homicide is that (a) about three out of every five handgun murder victims are related to or acquainted with their assailants, e.g., were friends, neighbors, spouses or ex-spouses, drinking buddies. By contrast, only 20 percent of all handgun killings are felony-related; and (b) almost half of all handgun killings are the result of an argument between such parties that got out of hand and culminated in the death of one of them (*The Banner,* 1987:3). These facts suggest that in many of the cases the assailant probably did not act out of a single-minded, unalterable intention to kill but was unduly influenced by the weapons effect (NBC Summer Showcase, 1988:22).

---

**Box 1.1 Experimental Evidence of a Weapons-Effect**

1. Angry college students could administer electric shocks to their partners by pressing a telegraph key on a table which was either empty or which sometimes had a shotgun and revolver on it. "The presence of the guns affected both the number of shocks the students gave their partners and how long they held the key down for each shock" (Berkowitz, 1968:19).
2. Children given toy guns to play with were more likely to press a button which they knew would cause their playmate's building blocks to collapse (Berkowitz, 1968).
3. Four- and five-year old children in nurseries were given different kinds of toys with which to play. Those who played with guns were more likely to display antisocial behavior (pushing, hitting) than children who were given airplanes and traditional toys. "Guns did more than lower the children's restraints against aggression; they seemed to pull out aggressive reactions that would not otherwise have occurred" (Berkowitz, 1968:20).
4. A rifle was placed in front of a carnival booth for some players (but not others) who threw wet sponges at a clown. Although the clown's deliberate insults had no effect, the presence of the rifle did: participants exposed to the gun threw more sponges at the clown than the other players (Berkowitz, 1981:12).
5. A pickup truck deliberately stalled at a green light. In one situation the truck had a rifle displayed in a gun rack that was clearly visible to the drivers immediately behind it; at other times there was no gun. The obstructed drivers who saw the rifle did more honking (the measure of aggression) than those not exposed to the gun (Berkowitz, 1981:12).

---

Between 1964-1974, 72 percent of the police officers feloniously killed in the line of duty were slain by handgun-wielding assailants, as were 75 percent of those killed in 1985 (*Crime Control Digest,* 1975:9; *Report to the Nation on Crime and Justice,* 1988:21). In the last decade handguns were used to murder over 100,000 people—about 25 handgun murders a day; and each year there are some 12,000 handgun suicides and 1,000 fatal handgun accidents (Gun Control Press Release, 1988; *New York Times,* 1986b). Except for President Kennedy's death, handguns were used in every attempted and completed assassination of American presidents or presidential candidates (Newton & Zimring, 1969:173). Bloch found that the fatality rate of aggravated assaults committed with handguns was 3-4 times greater than those committed with long guns or knives (Alviani & Drake, 1984:5). The apparent spread of handguns to the teenage population is one of the more recent and frightening developments in this area. Surveys in Baltimore revealed that as many as half of the male high school students have carried a handgun (NBC Summer Showcase, 1988:10).

The distinguishing attribute which makes handguns so well-adapted for criminal purposes and is the weapon of choice for crime commission is their easy *concealability* and attendant element of surprise. This explains why long guns are rarely used in robberies and that just 12 percent of all murders are committed with rifles or shotguns (Kleck, 1984c:191; *Report to the Nation on Crime and Justice,* 1988:20). The concealability of handguns makes them particularly convenient, useful and "just too handy" devices for the predatory criminal or as a means by which the law-abiding citizen thoughtlessly vents his or her anger in a fleeting moment of passion (ABC News Closeup, 1976:5-6). For these reasons and because handguns have little genuine hunting value,[2] it is an essential tenet of gun control that handguns have no legitimate function, have minimal if any real defensive value, and are "really designed as an efficient instrument for [only] one purpose: the killing and wounding of humans" (Riley, 1974:496, 506; Harris, 1976:58; Andrews, 1972:15).

## PREVALANCE OF GUN OWNERSHIP

The best source of information on the extent of gun ownership comes from various polls and surveys which have been conducted periodically since 1959 (Wright & Marston, 1975:94). In the 1973 National Opinion Research Corporation survey, 47 percent of the respondents (and 51% in 1977) said yes to the question "Do you happen to have in your home or garage any guns or revolvers?" (Wright, 1981:27). Two large national surveys, conducted separately by Decision Making Information and Cambridge Reports, found virtually identical proportions (23% and 24% respectively) of handgun ownership in American households (Wright, 1981:27).

These and other survey findings, which are remarkably consistent, lead to the following conclusions. About half of all U.S. households own some type of weapon, a figure that has remained basically unchanged since the 1959 Gallup poll (Wright & Marston, 1975:94). (The average number of firearms was 2.24 in gun-owning families according to the 1968 Harris poll). Almost one out of every four families owns a handgun. The proliferation of firearms is largely the result of gun-owning families adding to their inventory of weapons by acquiring handguns: whereas in 1959 only one-quarter of the gun-owning families had handguns, fully one-half of such families owned handguns in 1978 (Cook, 1983:50). In other words, the increase in gun ownership is accounted for by a greater concentration of handguns among families who already possess firearms, rather than to any rapid spread of handguns to a sector of the population that was previously gun-shy and unarmed (*Ten Myths About Gun Control,* 1987:3; Cook, 1983:80).

Determining how many (and what kinds of) firearms are in private hands is problematic because there is no federal law requiring that every gun be registered. Consequently, reliable estimates of firearms prevalence must be based on (a) annual domestic and imported gun production figures, with adjustments made for other sources and ways by which serviceable guns are put into or taken out of private circulation each year; and (b) survey data on the proportion of gun-owning households and their average number of weapons, information which is then applied and projected to the total number of households in the country (Wright, Rossi & Daly, 1983:26). In their report to the National Commission on the Causes and Prevention of Violence, Newton and Zimring (1969:4-7) estimated a private stock of 90 million firearms in 1968, of which 24 million were handguns. Some of the more recent "estimates" by proponents and opponents of gun control put the total gun count at closer to 200 million as of 1988, which purportedly includes 50-65 million handguns (Buchalter, 1988:7; Kluin, 1982:255). These figures, however, are probably somewhat fanciful because they are presented without any description of how they were arrived at and are often simply "rough guesses or wild surmise" by adversaries who exaggerate the oversupply of guns because it is in their respective interest to do so (Wright, Rossi & Daly, 1983:25). The number of weapons in private hands circa 1988 is reliably estimated to be about 150 million, of which about 50 million are handguns (Kluin, 1982:255). Moreover, there is a continuous build-up of private weaponry by virtue of new guns purchased from the pool of 2 million handguns and 4 million long guns which are manufactured domestically or imported from abroad annually (McClain, 1984:201; Danto, 1982:215).

Although firearms prevalence cannot be precisely established or categorized within a narrow range, the fact remains that "by whatever measure, the United States has an abundance of firearms—making it the most heavily armed industrial nation in the world (Newton & Zimring, 1969:7). It matters little, after all, whether there are currently 200 million firearms or, in fact, "only" 150 million. What matters is that such a vast magnitude of weapons among the general public makes gun "availability" a reality and is central to the gun control controversy.

# SATURDAY NIGHT SPECIALS

The term "Saturday Night Special" (SNS) was coined to describe cheap handguns which police noted were frequently used during weekend outbursts of criminal violence in poor neighborhoods of Detroit (Cook, 1981a:1736). There is considerable public interest in these ill-defined weapons—some places have moved to ban them—because they are commonly associated with street crime and, most notably, with the attempt on President Reagan's life (Bruce-Briggs, 1976:49). Since 1835, ten of the fifteen actual or would-be assassins chose small inexpensive pistols to assault presidents and other political figures (National Coalition to Ban Handguns). Do SNSs have a special relation to the commission of predatory crime? Are they the kind of weapons preferred and relied on by violent criminals, i.e., are SNSs "crime-guns."

The answer depends on what attribute or combination of characteristics are used to identify and define SNSs: quality of weapon, price, caliber, or barrel length. Price is considered relevant to the extent that many violent crimes are committed by persons who could not afford (or otherwise obtain) a more expensive weapon and might therefore be "priced out" of the criminal marketplace. Because poorly-constructed handguns are generally unreliable and inaccurate they are unsuitable for sporting purposes and have dubious value for self protection, making crime commission their logical chief application by default (Cook, 1981a:1736). Caliber provides only a rough indication of handgun size, whereas barrel length is a direct measure of size and hence of the weapon's concealability.

*Confiscation studies.* Most of what we know about SNSs as crime-guns comes from samples of firearms confiscated by the police. The advantage of examining police confiscations is that they offer the most concrete, tangible evidence on the characteristics of firearms used in connection with crime (Brill, 1977:26). In Project Identification, the first major study, the Bureau of Alcohol, Tobacco and Firearms (BATF) obtained information on all handguns (10,620) that were confiscated by 16 metropolitan police departments in the last six months of 1973. Project Identification defined SNSs as handguns with a price of under $50, of .32 caliber or less, *and* with a barrel length of 3 inches or less. Based on these criteria, the BATF found that 45 percent of the successfully traced handguns were SNSs (Wright et al., 1981:335; McClain, 1984:204).

Brill's survey of handguns confiscated by police in ten cities in 1975 focused on the price (under or over $60) and quality of the firearm, which were inferred from the manufacturer's brand name. For example, Smith & Wesson is known for making high quality, more expensive guns whereas R.G. Industries is a producer of inexpensive handguns. The prominence of moderate and high-priced handgun manufacturers in the confiscation sample led Brill to conclude that "inexpensive handguns are not used as weapons of violent crime any more often than other handguns" and to reject "the widespread notion that so-called SNSs are the favorite crime weapon" (Brill, 1977:49,53). Brill did not analyze the confiscated handguns in terms of their barrel length. But he does present data on handgun caliber in the 7 cities where such information was available, finding that 28-43 percent were *less* than .32 caliber, as were one-third for all cities combined (Brill, 1977:69-70). The BATF and most authorities, however, consider .32 caliber handguns as falling within the dividing line which separates small handguns from larger ones. Using .32 caliber or under as the cut-off point, "there is evidence of substantial involvement of SNSs in crime": between 48-71 percent of the handguns were in this size category, as were 54 percent for all cities combined (Brill, 1977:69).

*Confiscations and crime-guns.* There are two salient aspects of the confiscation studies which affect any assessment of the SNS role in the crime picture. (1) Police "confiscations" include not only firearms used to commit crime but also firearms simply found by the police while on patrol or voluntarily turned in by private citizens, i.e., all weapons recovered by police regardless of the circumstances or reasons for recovery. Between 20-25 percent of all firearms confiscated in Brill's survey, and probably a similar proportion in Project Identification, were unrelated to any crime (Brill, 1977:xvi; Wright et al., 1981:337-338). (2) Project Identification confiscation figures do not distinguish between handguns used *to* commit violent crime from situations where the only known crime was the "illegal possession" of the handgun itself. Brill (1977:24) found that 50-60 percent of all of his confiscations were for illegal possession (a "technicality"?) rather than for gun-related crimes. Because of such problems, confiscations can only provide an approximate, qualified reading of crime-gun characteristics and typology (Brill, 1977:26). Confiscation samples also may be biased toward detecting SNSs because many of the confiscated crime-handguns are found at the scene of a crime; and in making their escape, criminals may be more likely to discard cheap handguns rather than risk being caught with the weapon in their possession (Wright & Rossi, 1986:174).

*Concealability.* The one and only criterion consistently identified as the major component of crime-guns and the key to criminal misuse of handguns is concealability (Cook, 1981a:1745). "If a weapon is to be used for street crime activity, concealability is the first and foremost consideration of the acquirer and the length of the barrel of a particular handgun basically determines its concealability" (Alviani & Drake, 1983:12). There is an impressive array of research which documents the relationship between handgun concealability (small size) and crime.

- In Project Identification, 71 percent of the confiscated handguns had barrel lengths that were 3 inches or less, which is the boundary line for small, easily concealed firearms (Cook, 1981a:1744).

- A BATF study of guns confiscated in Washington, D.C., Chicago and Boston in 1976 is especially informative because it separated crime-handguns from other confiscations. Project CUE's principal finding was that:

  > the preponderance of small handguns with a barrel length of three inches or less is used for violent crime. More than two-thirds of the handguns in each violent crime category [homicide, robbery, aggravated assault] had this characteristic. Highly concealable handguns predominate in violent crime (Cook, 1981a:1743).

- Burr interviewed 808 Florida households and 277 felons in five state institutions during 1977. Although handgun caliber was not a factor which distinguished the two groups on gun ownership, concealability was: more than twice as many inmates (67%) owned handguns with barrel lengths 3 inches or under as did the household residents (30%) (Wright, Rossi & Daly, 1983:184-185). In a 1981 survey of Florida inmates convicted of homicide with a handgun, a slight majority (54%) owned handguns with similar barrel lengths (Coleman).

- In Brill's study, handgun calibers of .32 or less were associated with the majority of *all* robbery, *all* aggravated assault, and *all* narcotic offense confiscations (Brill, 1977:71).

*Wright-Rossi Felon Survey.* Based on interviews with 1874 male felons incarcerated in ten states throughout the country (the "Felon Survey" hereafter), Wright and Rossi concluded that:

> The idea that the SNS is a criminal's gun of choice turns out to be wrong. Our felon survey showed, overwhelmingly, that serious criminals both prefer to carry and actually do carry relatively large, big-bore, well-made handguns. No more than 1 in 7 [14%] of their handguns would qualify as small and cheap (Wright, 1988:34-35).

This finding and its implications, however, must be viewed with caution for a number of reasons.

All of the Felon Survey data refer to the "most-recent" handguns acquired by the men. It is possible that the firearms these offenders carried on a daily basis in anticipation of trouble or criminal opportunities may have been "other, smaller handguns that had been acquired at some earlier time (Wright & Rossi, 1986:173). Furthermore, the 14 percent SNS figure is based on the price and caliber of the most-recently owned handgun (Wright & Rossi, 1986:16,172). If barrel length were the sole yardstick, almost one-third (30%) of the felon's most-recent handguns would qualify as SNSs. The Felon Survey handgun information was based on what the offenders *said* and taken at face value; there was no empirical confirmation of their verbal responses to handgun questions. In describing the firearms they preferred and owned, the felons may have exaggerated the handgun characteristics in order to project a "macho" image to the field interviewers (Wright & Rossi, 1986:173). The Survey's most glaring limitation is that *it provides no information on crime-guns:* there was not attempt to link nor questions asked about the most-recent or previously owned handguns which were actually *used to commit a crime,* or the role of such weapons in the crimes for which they were incarcerated (Kleck, 1986a:303). Wright and Rossi recognize that their sample may be skewed toward more professional, career-oriented offenders by conceding that their sample of imprisoned felons is probably

> biased toward persons with longer and more violent careers in crime. If one-time, less violent, and/or juvenile offenders used smaller and different armaments from our more serious criminals, which also does not seem unlikely, then the Project Identification findings may well be accurate as a depiction of the "typical" crime handguns (Wright & Rossi, 1986:173).

## NOTES

[1]   The difference probably reflects the greater tendency for victims of more serious crime, such as those involving firearms, to be reported to the authorities.

[2]   Even under the most stringent gun control proposals, handguns could be used for target shooting at designated ranges.

# 2

# Gun Control

---

The debate over gun control has been a prominent feature of the political landscape since the early 1950s. The controversy is a battle over facts, political ideology, values, the Second Amendment, whether guns promote or deter crime, whether gun control laws work, why Americans want firearms, what criminals would do if handguns were unavailable to them, and how gun-owning citizens would respond to any attempt at disarmament (Cook, 1981b:64). At one time the weight of scholarly opinion was that stricter gun control measures were desirable and would be highly beneficial. But the conventional wisdom has shifted dramatically in the last decade, to the point where every major assumption behind gun control has been put under a microscope and critically analyzed. It can no longer be taken for granted that the case for gun control can be justified on scientific grounds alone or that the only thing standing in its way are the "gun nuts" and the National Rifle Association (Kaplan, 1986:1-2).

## APPROACHES TO GUN CONTROL

"Gun control" encompasses a broad range of legislative measures which place various restrictions on the acquisition, possession, use, sale and production of firearms. The laws, for example, may limit one's access to certain types of firearms or preclude certain types of people from acquiring firearms (Kleck, 1984a:24). The objective of gun control laws is to protect the public from the danger posed by and to reduce instances of firearm mishaps, reckless endangerment, and criminal misuse of weapons. This is accomplished by regulating the basic conditions of firearms usage and by separating legitimate from illegitimate gun users, i.e., keeping guns out of the "wrong hands."

*High-risk groups.* An obvious (and urgent) priority is to keep firearms out of the hands of persons known to be violence-prone, irresponsible or unreliable because they are prime candidates for firearms abuse. By virtue of their past actions or special status, people in certain "high-risk" groups are considered unqualified ("unfit") to be entrusted with lethal weapons. These *high-risk* groups, which the federal government and nearly every state prohibit from owning guns, typically include convicted felons, drug addicts, alcoholics, adjudicated mental incompetents, minors, fugitives from justice, and persons under indictment (Alviani & Drake, 1983). In practice, however, many of them are able to purchase guns from gun dealers because the laws are poorly enforced or because there was no effective mechanism for detecting their ineligibility before the sale was consummated (National Institute of Justice Crime File).

*Permissive licensing.* The policy for purchasing firearms (notably handguns) which exists in all but a few states is one of *permissive* licensing (Cook, 1983:82). The presumption behind permissive licensing is that citizens are legally *entitled* to own firearms so long as they do not fall into any of the proscribed high-risk groups. The process involved in qualifying for gun ownership—obtaining a license or permit-to-purchase, or completing an application coupled with a waiting period—is used to identify and weed out high-risk individuals; in effect, permissive licensure certifies that everyone else is automatically qualified to possess firearms and is a legitimate would-be gun owner (Magaddino & Medoff, 1984:230; Kleck, 1986b:40). After complying with the procedural formalities of permissive licensing, the licensing authority has little if any discretion to withhold approval; applicants must be issued a license, permit, identification card, or other necessary document which allows them to purchase and take possession of a firearm from a gun dealer (Cook & Blose, 1981:86-87).

*Restrictive licensing.* Some jurisdictions have *restrictive* (or "discretionary") licensing policies, under which prospective gun buyers are not entitled to own a firearm simply because they are not a "certified lunatic" or in any of the other prohibited classes. Instead, only people who are able to demonstrate a special need or compelling reason for having a gun are issued a license. And "home defense" or self protection is usually not a bonafide special need, because doing so would make guns readily available to one and all. Licenses to purchase firearms are thus restricted to persons in narrowly defined categories, on a demonstrable "need-to-have" basis, which entails fingerprinting, photographing and a thorough background investigation by law enforcement officials (Alviani & Drake, 1983:31). Even then, there is no "right" to be issued a license. The licensing authority or police[1] board has the discretion to deny a permit for whatever reasons they deem appropriate, e.g., the applicant lacked "good moral character," some other aspect of their life was suspect, or simply because the reason given for needing a firearm was not considered important or good enough. To have the best chance of obtaining licensing approval, citizens must be able to convince the board that carrying or keeping a gun at home or at work is essential to their well-being, is job-related, or necessary for conducting business (Kaplan, 1984:xxviii; Magaddino & Marshall, 1984:230-231).

## THE GUN CONTROL CONTROVERSY

As things now stand, almost anyone can obtain a handgun because the majority of people live in areas with permissive licensing policies, no special license or permit is needed to own a handgun in some places, and most of the 20,000 gun ordinances in the country are not directed at curtailing handgun ownership among the general public (Bruce-Briggs, 1976:43). The focus of the gun control debate is on *stricter* government regulation of handguns because they dominate the gun crime statistics (relative to long guns) and therefore constitute the gun problem in America. The goal of the gun control movement is to drastically reduce the possession of handguns among the population at large—among ordinary, law-abiding citizens who are "legitimate" gun owners.

Gun control is a call for:

(a) the restrictive licensing of all handguns as the norm,

(b) banning SNS-type handguns, possibly through prohibiting or discouraging their production,

(c) tightening the screening purchasing procedures in all existing gun laws—preferably through federal legislation—so that high-risk persons do not slip through the cracks, and

(d) prohibiting any private citizen from possessing "assault" weapons (Bruce-Briggs, 1976:42).

A surprising number of convicted felons and other prohibited category people obtain handguns in over-the-counter purchases on a "no questions asked" basis. Toward these ends, organizations like Handgun Control (see Box 2.1) and the National Coalition to Ban Handguns are committed to taking handguns out of general circulation and taking on the National Rifle Association by developing broadly based constituencies of their own. Because long guns (except "assault" rifles) are not a priority of gun control advocates, they would continue to be readily available under permissive licensing (Moore, 1981:93). Targeting handguns has the tactical advantage of blunting criticism and neutralizing opposition from America's 20 million hunters and sportsmen, by providing reassurance that it is not *their* firearms, rights, or activities which would be affected by "gun control." And surveys indicate that public opinion may be sympathetic to some types of handgun restrictions, owing to the "fear of crime" which handguns generate and their association with political assassination (Kleck, 1984c:168-169).

---

**Box 2.1 Handgun Control's Legislative Agenda** (below) is a blueprint of mainstream gun control objectives.

- *a waiting period and background check* to screen out illegal handgun purchasers such as convicted felons and drug users.
- *a mandatory jail sentence* for using a handgun in the commission of a crime.
- *a license-to-carry law*, requiring a special license to carry a handgun outside one's home or place of business.
- *a ban on the manufacture and sale of snub-nosed handguns*, the Saturday Night Specials used in two-thirds of handgun crime.
- *restriction on the sale of assault rifles*, paramilitary weapons like those used in the 1989 Stockton massacre (discussed later) and the 1983 McDonald's mass killings in California.
- *a ban on the manufacture and sale of plastic handguns*, which make metal detectors and airport screening devices useless.

Source: Adapted from Handgun Control pamphlet *One Million Strong,* undated.

---

*Rationale of handgun control.* The rationale for purging society of handguns runs along the following lines. Much of the present gun legislation is in the category of reasonable social precautions or is geared to the known criminal element and other deviant groups (Wright, 1988:26). The "wrong hands" for handguns, however, are not only those of the more identifiable high-risk groups who are prohibited from owning firearms. It is impossible to distinguish, in advance, between those who will and won't misuse handguns because there is no clear dividing line separating "real criminals" from ordinary citizens who, while in a highly emotional state, resort to handgun violence to settle an argument or vent their anger.

By cracking down on handgun availability throughout society, many of these tragedies could be prevented, and many law-abiding citizens would avoid "becoming" criminals as a result of the weapons-effect phenomenon. In addition, the more accessible handguns are, the more likely it is that many of them will fall into the wrong hands of the criminal element through theft and loss, as an estimated 275,000 weapons do each year (Jacobs, 1986:5-6). To summarize, handgun control would dry up a source of crime-guns for street criminals, and would prevent some (admittedly violence-prone) law-abiding citizens from turning a weapon of self-protection into a crime-gun (Kleck et al., 1982:21). But is it fair to penalize the entire population in order to prevent some small, marginal number of street criminals and domestic offenders from engaging in criminal violence—only 1 out of every 5400 handguns will ever be used to commit a crime? (Kleck, 1984b:132). Would society actually be safer, better served and better off under restrictive gun control? Might not handgun availability be as important a factor in crime deterrence as it is in crime commission?

## THE NATIONAL RIFLE ASSOCIATION

With almost 3 million members, an annual budget of $70 million, and a staff of lobbyists in the nation's capital, the National Rifle Association (NRA) is regarded as the most powerful and effective anti-gun control organization in the country (*Time*, 1981; *New York Times*, 1988c; Elias, 1987:42). As a single-issue pressure group dedicated to hard-line political action, the NRA's main arguments are that gun control is a violation of the Second Amendment "right to bear arms," will ultimately lead to registration and confiscation, and that handgun restrictions deprive citizens of the means of self-protection without hampering criminals access to weapons: "When guns are outlawed, only outlaws will have guns" (*Newsweek*, 1982).

*NRA a "magnum" force.* The NRA's seemingly sure-fire formula for success involves contributing generously to the re-election of politicians who are pro-gun candidates and working tirelessly to discredit and defeat those who show the slightest sign of being gun-control sympathizers. The methods employed by the NRA include keeping tabs on the voting records of members of Congress, letter-writing campaigns, having NRA members appear at legislative hearings, mobilizing a network of affiliated groups nationwide, and a "political victory fund" used to remove from office politicians who do not endorse the NRA party line (*Time*, 1981).

When the BATF proposed revisions in federal law that would have made it easier to trace crime-guns, within two months the NRA marshaled 350,000 letters to the Bureau, claiming that the proposal was a veiled effort to confiscate all firearms from the American people (*Time*, 1981). The man responsible for the idea was the object of character assassination and harrassing phone calls, and the proposal was promptly dropped (*Time*, 1981). When hearings were held in April 1981 in Jefferson City, Missouri, concerning proposed legislation to ban private handgun sales, 2 people showed up to testify in favor of the ban; the NRA got 6,000 faithful to converge on the capital opposing the measure (*Time*, 1981).

Former South Dakota Senator George McGovern originally favored banning small handguns but subsequently caved in to NRA pressure and ended up supporting efforts to deregulate firearm purchases. Unforgiving of the Senator's initial transgression, the NRA threw its support and $30,000 behind pro-gun rival James Abdnor, and McGovern was defeated for re-election. The same fate befell former Sen. Birch Bayh of Indiana (*Time,* 1981). Gerald Ford initially favored banning SNSs but, in his 1976 presidential bid, backed down upon recognizing the wisdom of not incurring the NRA's wrath or losing its members' votes (*Time,* 1981). The target of a $205,000 NRA campaign opposing his bid for the democratic presidential nomination, Edward Kennedy spent much of his time disclaiming NRA reports that he wanted to confiscate all hunting firearms (*Time,* 1981). In the 1984 Congressional campaigns, the NRA contributed $1.4 million to its "friends," thereby tipping the balance in many close calls for re-election (*U.S. News & World Report,* 1986b).

Local politicians may be in a somewhat better position to withstand NRA pressure tactics because, as Morton Grove village trustee Don Sneider puts it, "I don't need NRA finances to get into office" (*Newsweek,* 1982). However, the NRA's influence at the grass roots level should not be underestimated because "the NRA has developed supporters in each community, those who can effectively lobby not only federal officials but local and state officials as well" (*Newsweek,* 1981).

*NRA no longer bullet-proof?* Separate recent developments may yet prove that the NRA is not invincible. For the first time since it was founded in 1871, the NRA is facing serious organized opposition from national gun control lobbies which seem to be gaining members and legislative clout around the country (*New York Times,* 1988c). Handgun Control, the NRA's most formidable competitor, has 200,000 dues-paying members, an annual budget of $3 million, and to achieve its program objectives has adopted the successful strategy and methods of its nemesis (Buchalter, 1988:4). Handgun Control does not object to handgun ownership per se but advocates a national "waiting period" before one is allowed to purchase a firearm, so that police can check the applicant's background (*One Million Strong*). By contrast, the National Coalition to Ban Handguns is adamantly opposed to the private ownership of handguns under any circumstances, believing that waiting periods and similar screening devices are halfway measures which cannot halt the criminal violence caused by handguns (*U.S. News & World Report,* 1980).

Besides encountering opposition from new sources, there is a growing rift between the NRA and one of its staunchest and oldest allies, the police. Some officers and law enforcement groups are coming to see weak gun control laws as a direct threat to their safety and the NRA's rigidity on the subject as being insensitive to police welfare. In particular, the NRA managed to offend the police community by its opposition to waiting periods and to banning plastic guns, machine guns, and armor-piercing ("cop-killer") ammunition[2] that can penetrate bulletproof vests worn by police *U.S. News & World Report,* 1987a). Police disagreement and disenchantment with the NRA over such matters—by speaking out and by their presence in the capital at a critical period—helped prevent the NRA from substantially weakening the Gun Control Act of 1968 (*U.S. News & World Report,* 1986b).

# NOTES

[1]  While they are active public servants, police are of course exempted from such restrictive requirements; but upon retirement or entering another occupation, they would be subject to the same restrictive licensing requirements.

[2]  As part of a crime control package of laws enacted in 1984, federal felons who use body armor-piercing ammunition in the commission of a crime face a minimum mandatory prison sentence.

# 3

# Federal Gun Legislation

---

In the 1920s and 1930s the public's fear of crime was focused on the wave of gangsterism, personified by John Dillinger, and mayhem that was then sweeping the country. In response, the National Firearms Act of 1934 sought to inhibit the sale or private possession of machine guns, sawed-off shotguns and silencers—which had acquired the reputation as gangster weapons ("crime guns") of that era—by levying a heavy tax[1] on commerce in these weapons. (The Roosevelt Administration originally tried to impose a national licensing system of all firearms, but that effort was squashed by the NRA.) The Federal Firearms Act of 1938 was aimed at regulating a broader spectrum of firearms than the specialized gangster-weapons of its predecessor. It required that all individuals and companies in the firearms business be federally licensed and prohibited dealers from selling firearms to known criminals. In doing the latter, Congress, for the first time, set forth categories of persons who were, by definition, "unfit to possess firearms." (Shields, 1981:77). The 1938 legislation was steered through Congress by the NRA, whose main concern was that the emerging federal interest in shaping gun policy was not carried too far. While limited in scope, these two laws solidified the federal government's role in firearms control policy and were the immediate precursors of the Gun Control Act of 1968 (Zimring, 1975:138-139; Riley, 1974:508).

## THE GUN CONTROL ACT OF 1968

*Major provisions.* The culmination of five years of public debate and bitter opposition by the NRA, the Gun Control Act of 1968 (GCA 68) was hastily passed by an aroused Congress in the wake of the assassinations[2] of Robert F. Kennedy and Martin Luther King, Jr. (Kates, 1986a:49). The GCA 68 had three major provisions and objectives.

(a) *Banning interstate firearm sales.* The centerpiece of the Act was the licensing of manufacturers, importers and gun dealers ("firearm

19

entrepreneurs") and prohibiting gun dealers from selling firearms or ammunition to out-of-state residents.[3] The intended effect of these provisions was to reduce the flow of weapons from one jurisdiction to another, i.e., to prevent "leakage" (Zimring, 1975:149) (see Closeup 3.1). Stringent (restrictive) gun codes in one area were undermined by the easy accessibility of weapons in nearby areas with more permissive or looser regulations. Banning interstate firearm transfers to unlicensed individuals (private parties) was the mechanism for helping the states and localities to enforce their own gun control requirements, especially by giving jurisdictions with tough gun control measures a chance to work (Zimring, 1975:149; Kleck, 1986b:50). Since the language of this provision required individuals to appear in person to buy a gun, the CGA 68 incorporated a national ban against purchasing any firearm by mail-order. An earlier federal statute only banned using the mails to obtain *concealable* weapons, which did nothing to prevent people like Lee Harvey Oswald from receiving rifles via mail-order on an almost anonymous basis (Cook, 1983:81). A Senate Subcommittee studying mail-order guns sold to Washington, D.C. residents (a very restrictive jurisdiction) found that "criminals, immature juveniles, and other irresponsible persons were using the relative secrecy of the mail order/common carrier method of obtaining firearms, because they could not purchase guns under the laws in their own jurisdiction" (Zimring, 1975:145).

(b) *Denying firearms to prohibited classes.* The Act barred the sale of firearms and ammunition to designated groups considered too unreliable, irresponsible or potentially dangerous to own them. These prohibited groups include:

- convicted felons
- fugitives from justice
- persons under felony indictment
- drug users (including marijuana) and narcotics addicts
- minors[4]
- adjudicated mental incompetents·
- individuals involuntarily committed to mental institutions
- illegal aliens
- persons dishonorably discharged from the armed forces

(c) *Restricting imports.* The Act prohibited the importation of firearms unless they were considered "particularly suitable for *sporting purposes*," a phrase that was not defined in the legislation but clearly did not affect long guns (Zimring, 1975:149). By adopting this sporting-test, Congress sought to control the foreign influx of Saturday Night Specials, which were perceived as being too cheap, too plentiful and too closely tied to crime commission (Magaddino & Medoff, 1984:243).

## CLOSEUP 3.1: FIREARMS LEAKAGE

With so many states and municipalities regulating firearms acquisition in one way or another, why the continued clamor for yet another federal law on the subject? Because they haven't been very successful. Part of the reason that the "unfathomable labyrinth" of 20,000 gun laws and ordinances are often ineffective is because they are so easily evaded by purchasing firearms in other jurisdictions which have a more open policy toward gun ownership (Riley, 1974:512). "Serious efforts at state and local regulation have consistently been frustrated by the flow of firearms from one state to another," Newton and Zimring noted in their report to the Violence Commission (Newton & Zimring, 1969:95). According to this perspective, the only way to remedy the "will travel-have gun" problem is by adopting a strong national firearms policy that can be uniformly applied across all states (Wright, 1988:27). Hence, "the primary justification for federal controls is the interstate leakage of firearms" (Kleck, 1986b:50). An essential aim of the CGA 68 was to prevent leakage—thereby reinforcing existing state controls—by prohibiting gun dealers from selling weapons to out-of-state residents.

There is ample evidence to support the hypothesis that leakage severely weakens gun control measures. New York's Sullivan Law involves meeting the special-need criterion before anyone may legally obtain a firearm (Zimring, 1975:177). Largely because of this, only half a dozen of the 60,000 permit holders in New York City have ever used their guns to commit crime. Yet the city's rate of handgun crime continued to soar because of leakage from Southern states, where truck drivers passing through could pick up "junk guns" costing $20 apiece and resell them in Harlem for three times the price (Andrews, 1972:15-16). Two-thirds of the handguns confiscated in New York City came from outside the state, and a majority of the estimated 2 million handguns in circulation there were probably illegally obtained (Kleck, 1984c:194). A 1973 BATF study which traced a sample of handguns used to commit crime in New York state found that only 5 percent were originally purchased within the state; one-quarter of the New York crime guns came from South Carolina alone (Zimring, 1975:181).

Surveys show that the leakage story is much the same in other places with tough gun laws, such as Massachusetts where an estimated 87 percent of all crime-guns came from outside the state (Zimring, 1975:175,181). After the 1967 Detroit riots, Michigan residents "stocked up" on handguns by flocking to Toledo, Ohio, once known as the "gun capital of the Midwest," because firearms could be readily purchased not only at gun shops but also at jewelry stores, supermarkets and gasoline stations with no questions asked. At one time, 8 states did not have any law against felons purchasing firearms, and Texas residents could carry handguns either concealed or openly without a permit (Riley, 1974:512-513).

*Role of BATF.* Administration of the CGA 68 became the responsibility of the Bureau of Alcohol, Tobacco & Firearms (BATF) (Zimring, 1975:144). The Bureau's *regulatory*[5] activities include the process of licensing applicants and monitoring the records of gun dealers in order to enforce the ban against selling firearms to nonresidents or prohibited groups. Pursuant to the latter, Bureau agents perform "compliance checks" and audits by periodically inspecting dealer records to confirm that licensees are maintaining the required forms and information for all weapons received and sold. Bureau agents were authorized to make unannounced visits, as often as they liked, to gun dealers to verify that gun dealers were operating in accordance with the federal law. The records and transaction forms themselves, however, were retained by the individual dealers and thus decentralized, which was a conscious decision by Congress in order to avoid any semblance or charge that the Act was a ploy for implementing firearms registration. If the BATF turned up a pattern of willful violations of the Act, dealers could lose their licenses. But with just 600 inspectors at its disposal to keep tabs on some 250,000 licensed dealers, the Bureau's ability to effectively oversee dealer record-keeping was severely hampered (*Newsweek,* 1988a; Zimring, 1975:149,158).

*Loopholes in law.* The GCA 68 contained certain loopholes which thwarted each of its major objectives. The Act did not ban the importation of SNS *parts.* Importers exploited this loophole by setting up "cottage industries" in this country—garages and churches were converted into makeshift factories—for the purpose of assembling the foreign parts into serviceable Specials (Gettinger, 1980:17). The number of imported handgun parts soared from 18,000 units in 1968 to over one million by 1972, and their sales volume increased steadily from $700,000 in 1969 to over $7 million by 1982 (Zimring, 1975:169-170; Alviani & Drake, 1983:22). In addition, the Act placed no restrictions whatsoever on the *domestic* production of SNSs; for example, in 1974 half of the 1.9 million handguns manufactured here failed to meet the Bureau's sporting-purpose criterion, based on barrel-length (*New York Times,* 1975b). American firearm producers were quick to fill the gap left by imported SNSs. Within a few years, domestic firms were manufacturing far more SNSs than the number of SNSs imported in 1967 (the peak year); and domestic handgun production more than doubled between 1968 and 1981 (Riley, 1974:511; Zimring, 1975:169-170).

*No effective verification.* The most glaring loophole was the absence of any effective mechanism for implementing the ban against selling firearms to out-of-state residents and high-risk groups. It was unlawful for dealers to transfer weapons to such individuals only if the dealer *knew or had reason to believe* that the customer was ineligible to receive guns. Dealers were only required to "verify" the customer's residence and age by inspecting any common document showing this information on its face—like a driver's license or social security card—which constituted satisfactory identification for the purpose of authorizing the sale (Cook & Blose, 1981:84; Magaddino & Medoff, 1984:242).

It was a relatively simple matter for any ineligible buyer to produce a false driver's license, other bogus identification, or have someone else buy a gun for them. Other than this rudimentary screening, there was no verification procedure at all for weeding out customers who were convicted felons, drug addicts, mentally deranged and the like, i.e., the Act relied upon the "honor system."

Every customer merely had to sign, under penalty of perjury, Federal Form 4473 attesting that they were not in any of the ineligible categories, and in many places they could then leave the gun store armed to the hilt (*New York Times,* 1975a). The risk of getting caught while making an illegal gun purchases was remote precisely because there was no reliable method for detecting their misrepresentation (like a waiting period) either prior to or at the point of sale. The threat posed to customers for violating the law was indirect and after-the-fact: if a person who used false ID, subterfuge, or lied on Form 4733 was subsequently apprehended with a firearm, the record-keeping system made it possible to determine if the suspect was guilty of illegal possession and violating the Act itself, a separate offense punishable by up to five years imprisonment (Zimring, 1975:153). Thus, in practice the Act did little to deter ineligible persons from obtaining weapons through over-the-counter purchases (Zimring, 1975:152). A final limitation of the Act was that it did not apply to *unlicensed*[6] individuals: private citizens (nondealers) could sell or transfer weapons to anyone they pleased without having to keep a record of the transaction or verifying the recipient's age or residence (Kleck, 1986b:52; Cook & Blose, 1981:84). This omission was a potentially serious blow to gun control since half of all handgun acquisitions come from private or second-hand sources ("street sales") (Riley, 1974:510).

## FIREARMS OWNERS PROTECTION ACT OF 1986

The NRA deeply resented the "unreasonable curbs" which the CGA 68 placed on gun purchases by law-abiding citizens. The Act's burdensome paperwork requirements, surprise inspections by the BATF, and alleged harassment of gun dealers over minor record-keeping violations were also sore spots which the NRA resolved to do something about at the right time. The NRA decided to mount a concentrated effort to roll back the 68 Act after the landslide election of President Reagan, himself an NRA member and (even after being shot by Hinckley) a staunch opponent of gun control (*New York Times*, 1975a). This NRA objective, in the works for six years with Reagan Administration support, was realized by passage of the 1986 Firearms Owners Protection Act (FOPA), the first significant change in federal gun policy in nearly two decades.

The gun lobby had no trouble getting its proposals through the Senate, which would have dismantled the GCA 68 by repealing its ban against interstate firearm sales. It was at this point, however, that police groups and the widows of slain officers joined forces with Handgun Control and started to speak out against the NRA-sponsored legislation (*U.S. News & World Report*, 1986b). A coalition of 10 national police organizations denounced the Senate bill as posing "an immediate and unwarranted threat to the law enforcement community" (*New York Times*, 1986a). In a desperate move to salvage the 68 Act while warding off conservative pressure, the House Judiciary Committee drafted an alternative bill (subsequently enacted) that preserved the existing restrictions on interstate firearm sales but acquiesced to virtually all other NRA demands for markedly weakening the 68 Act. In the end, the NRA's muscle and its $1.6 million lobbying campaign was mightier than police protests, Handgun Control or the crusading voice of Sarah Brady—the wife of former White House Press Secretary James Brady (who was shot by Hinckley) (*New York Times*, 1986c).

The Firearms Owners Protection Act made it easier to buy, sell and transport firearms across state lines (Public Law 99-308). It:

- reduced record-keeping requirements of gun dealers, limited government inspection (which must be announced in advance) to once a year, made it easier to become a licensed gun dealer, and made record-keeping violations a misdemeanor instead of a felony (Dole, 1986:221; *Newsweek*, 1988a).

- lifted the ban against transporting firearms across state lines. Handguns and long guns may now be transported between states provided they are unloaded and not "readily accessible," e.g., are in the glove compartment or car trunk.

- allowed gun dealers to transfer firearms to their "personal collection," from which weapons may be sold without keeping any records of these transactions.

- permitted the mail-order purchase of ammunition, and the interstate sales of long guns (but not handguns) provided that such purchase is legal in the buyer's home state.

The only issue on which gun control advocates prevailed was in retaining the ban against interstate sales of handguns. And in a last-minute amendment, Congress prohibited any further sale of machine guns to the public (*U.S. News & World Report*, 1988a). Those already owning "Tommy" guns at the time could retain them legally but were barred from selling them (*New York Times*, 1986c). The combined changes and effects of the FOPA have, arguably, made it easier for criminals to acquire and transport weapons and make it more difficult for the BATF to trace guns used in crime (*U.S. News & World Report*, 1986a).

## THE BRADY BILL

> Q. "Who would argue against legislation that could keep criminals and crazies from buying a handgun? Who would argue against legislation that could have prevented John W. Hinckley from buying the Saturday Night Special that injured President Reagan and gravely wounded James S. Brady, his press secretary?" (*New York Times*, 1987b).
>
> A. The NRA.

In 1988 the proposed Handgun Violence Prevention Act, or Brady Bill as it was informally referred to (named after James Brady) was defeated by the NRA. Partially inspired by Sarah Brady and the flagship legislation of Handgun Control Inc., the Brady Bill would have imposed a mandatory national 7-day waiting period on *handgun* sales This interval would give police an opportunity to conduct a background investigation on prospective purchasers and would provide a "cooling-off" period during which they might change their mind about wanting a gun, thereby preventing some crimes of passion from occurring. Instead of taking the customer's word for it, the Brady amendment established a procedure for verifying whether the customer was a felon, non-resident, mentally incompetent (see Exhibit 3A) or otherwise ineligible for firearms, i.e., for corroborating the information in the customer's sworn statement, federal Form 4733 (Elias, 1987:42). The national waiting period's verification system would put teeth into the CGA 68 by stopping leakage from non-waiting period states.

*Could it have stopped Hinckley?* Much of the publicity in support of the Brady bill was that had a nationwide waiting period been in effect earlier, a background check might have revealed that Hinckley lied on the form (a felony) about being a Texas resident when he purchased the handguns in the Dallas pawnshop (*USA Today*, 1987a). "Had police been given an opportunity to discover the lie, John Hinckley may well have been in jail instead of on his way to Washington" (*What You Should Know About the Brady Bill*). In addition, "if Texas had had a waiting period, Hinckley would not have been able to purchase the guns after the Nashville incident[7] because the requisite background check would have divulged previous criminal offenses." But because there was no waiting period or background check, the pawnshop dealer who sold him the weapon had no way of knowing or reason to suspect that Hinckley was a nonresident or had a criminal record or history of mental illness (*New York Times,* 1985a).

---

**Exhibit 3A**

One day in the summer of 1987, Larry Dale, 36, "stepped into a Tulsa grocery store and started shooting. Shouting 'Go to God,' Dale fired 21 hollow-point bullets. One man died after being hit with 14; another was wounded. The day before, at a store across the street, Dale got his .22 calibre revolver by plunking down just $139 and filling out honor-system forms stating he was not a felon or crazy. Dale lied on both counts. He'd been convicted on a weapons charge in 1984. And he confided to a court-appointed psychologist that 'since 1979 he has believed he is God.' "

Source: *USA Today,* August 2, 1988, p.1A.

---

*Waiting period not new.* Waiting periods for handguns were not a new idea or practice, nor the first time that Congress had considered the matter. In the early 1980s Edward Kennedy and Peter Rodino proposed a three-week waiting period for handguns, and in 1985 the Senate rejected a waiting period by a wide margin (*Time,* 1981). In recommending a national waiting period in 1982, the Attorney General's Task Force on Violent Crime aptly noted that felons, drug addicts and mental defectives "are not the best risk for the honor system." By 1988, 22 states had waiting periods for handguns, whether expressly labeled as such or as an intrinsic aspect of obtaining a gun license, permit or owner's identification card (Cook & Blose, 1981:85; *Time,* 1988b; *New York Times,* 1987b). These waiting periods ranged from only two or three days—perhaps not enough time for an adequate investigation or to check out all applications—to up to two weeks in Tennessee, Hawaii and California (Cook & Blose, 1981:85). The Brady Bill would have standardized the interval between purchasing a handgun and its actual receipt, and prevented buyers in waiting-period states from obtaining guns by going to no-waiting-period states.

*Logistics of waiting period.* Under the Brady proposal, prospective buyers continue to fill out Form 4473 certifying that they are not disqualified by federal law from acquiring handguns. Gun dealers would have to send a copy of this document to the chief local law enforcement official in the area. The police would have the option of verifying the information therein; the background check itself was not mandatory, although it was expected that they would conduct investigations in most cases. The thoroughness and mechanics of the investigation were left to the discretion of local responsible authorities. Depending on the outcome of the background check, the police would notify the gun dealer whether the handgun sale was approved or disapproved. If the dealer did not receive word within the 7 days, the transfer could automatically be consummated, i.e., silence conferred approval (Magaddino & Medoff, 1984:231). To alleviate NRA fears that a uniform waiting period would be used to create a national registry of firearms, the Brady Bill required the police to destroy their copies of the forms within 60 days after the sale was approved (*Newsweek*, 1988b).

*1988—Brady Bill bites the dust.* The Brady Bill received strong support from several quarters, including the police community (Elias, 1987:42). President Reagan himself praised the notion of a waiting period and cited how well it had worked in California when he was governor. An earlier (1981) Gallup poll found that 9 out of 10 Americans favored a waiting period for handgun purchases (*New York Times*, 1987b). But the amendment was fiercely opposed by the NRA, which warned its members that the bill was the beginning of "the step-by-step process where the Second Amendment right to keep and bear arms becomes a privilege" (*Criminals Don't Wait*, 1988; *USA Today*, 1988d). The pro-control forces, which spent $200,000 lobbying for the measure, were no match for the NRA's political clout, $4 million anti-Brady campaign, and aggressive lobbying tactics.[8] With national elections just around the corner, even many Congress members who favored the proposal could not afford to vote their conscience. The House of Representatives bowed to NRA pressure and killed the Brady Bill by a vote of 228 to 182 (*Time*, 1988b; *U.S. News & World Report*, 1988b).

*1991—Brady Bill not a dead issue.* Three years after its 1988 defeat, the Brady Bill was once again on the congressional agenda, but this time its chances for passage seemed greatly improved. The reason for such optimism was that Ronald Reagan, in a speech at George Washington University on March 28, 1991, announced he had changed his mind and was now in favor of a nationwide law requiring a 7-day waiting period for purchasing handguns. "I am going to say it in clear, unmistakable language. I support the Brady Bill and I urge Congress to enact it without further delay. With the right to bear arms comes a great responsibility to use caution and common sense on handgun purchases" (*USA Today*, 1991). The former president's bold endorsement was viewed by gun control advocates as providing the necessary momentum and much-needed boost for enactment of the 7-day waiting period. And President Bush, a lifelong member of the NRA, who is on record opposing stricter gun control, indicated a willingness to reconsider his position on the Brady Bill in exchange for political concessions in connection with his proposed crime package legislation. It remains to be seen whether, in the words of Rep. Edward Feighan, the Brady Bill's "victory is assured," or, as seems more likely, the measure still faces an uphill battle (*New York Times*, 1991).

**CLOSE-UP 3.2: OPPOSING VIEWPOINTS
ON WAITING PERIODS**

*Against waiting periods.* Waiting periods:
- will be circumvented by criminals because they will obtain firearms through secondary sources and the booming interstate gun-smuggling business (*USA Today*, 1988c). "Drug dealers or anyone intent on committing a crime won't register or wait for anyone's permission to get a gun" (*USA Today*, 1988d). The Felon Survey concluded that retail sales play a minor role as direct sources of criminal handguns.
- create a massive, costly bureaucracy to implement the background investigations. Police departments, which are so strapped now that many can't investigate burglary reports, would be diverted from the business of fighting crime "to the unrewarding task of snooping into the private lives of law-abiding citizens buying guns through licensed firearms dealers" (*Criminals Don't Wait*, 1988:2-3).
- don't work. Although almost half of the states require background checks on all handgun transfers, studies reveal that "there is no convincing empirical evidence that a police check on handgun buyers reduces violent crime rates." For example, homicide rates remained unchanged in states which introduced or extended their waiting period times between 1965 to 1985; nor were there any differences in the homicide rates when cities with and without waiting periods were compared (*Criminals Don't Wait*, 1988:6-8; *USA Today*, 1987a).
- would hinder law-abiding citizens from protecting themselves against crime. "Criminals don't wait, why should you"? (*Criminals Don't Wait*, 1988:12).
- lend themselves to bureaucratic abuse. In some waiting period jurisdictions, countless applications for handguns have been mysteriously "lost," and customers are subjected to endless roadblocks to discourage them from gun ownership. In New Jersey, the police refused to issue any permits for one year because the FBI balked at doing the fingerprint checks they requested.
- are based on the unwarranted assumption that newly purchased firearms are used to commit violent crime. However, the Brill survey found that just 2.1 percent of the handguns traced to crime were under one month old, which is four times longer than the Brady Bill waiting period. And since an estimated 75 percent of gun buyers already own firearms, a waiting period would be irrelevant for those bent on committing violent crime (*Criminals Don't Wait*, 1988:4-5,9).

*Waiting periods are needed.* "Contrary to the assertions of some, convicted criminals do attempt to purchase handguns through legitimate channels of commerce" (*What You Should Know About the Brady Bill*). It is surprising how many felons use their real name but lie to gun dealers about being convicted felons (*New York Times*, 1985b). The Felon Survey found that almost one-fifth (17%) of the gun-owning felons got their most recent handgun from retail transactions (Wright, 1986). The experience of many jurisdictions confirm that waiting periods *do* work: Maryland's one-week waiting period stopped 732 felons from purchasing handguns in 1986. California's two-week delay keeps guns out of the hands of 1,200-1,500 criminals a year. In the 19 years that New Jersey has required background checks, over 10,000 convicted felons were caught trying to purchase handguns (*USA Today,* 1988d; *What You Should Know About the Brady Bill;* Buchalter, 1988:4). In Memphis, Tennessee, a waiting period screens out about 50 applicants a month, most of whom have criminal records. With a 72-hour cooling-off period, Dade County (Fla.) nonetheless experienced an 80 percent increase in their murder rate between 1975-1980—possibly because it is so easy to buy handguns without waiting in nearby Broward County, less than an hour away (Coleman).

Harvard University's Mark Moore estimates that as many as 90,000 handguns a year may be sold to criminals and others who are prohibited by federal law from having them (*What You Should Know About the Brady Bill*). A national waiting period could impact the problem of unsavory gun dealers who knowingly sell guns to unqualified customers. A no-exceptions mandatory waiting period is even more urgent than mandatory sentences because the goal is to prevent violent crime *from occurring,* rather than just closing the barn door after the damage has been done. The inconvenience of a waiting period is no greater than that involved in getting a driver's license or qualifying for a credit card. Would a delay of seven days be so burdensome to the public as to outweigh the threat posed to the community by criminals, for whom the same delay is a salient stumbling block for obtaining the tools of their trade (*USA Today*, 1987a). Could a seven-day delay, in any realistic sense, deprive law-abiding citizens of the opportunity to ward off crime? A waiting period is obviously no guarantee that criminals will not get handguns elsewhere or preempt suicides and crimes of passion, but isn't it a step in the right direction? Combined with other remedies, like mandatory sentences, might not they put a dent in handgun crime and handgun deaths? (Handgun Violence Protection Act of 1987).

Perhaps the most compelling testimony for a national waiting period comes from James Wright, the senior author of the Felon Survey whose findings and conclusions have been widely cited by the NRA as lending scientific credibility to the gun lobby's position. In the same article in which Wright expresses doubts about gun control, he states that waiting periods "seem reasonable since there are very few legitimate purposes to which a firearm might be put [including self-protection] that would be thwarted if the user had to wait a few days, or even a few weeks, to get the gun" (Wright, 1988:26). A customer in the same Florida gun shop where Arthur Kane bought his crime-handgun had the same sentiment: "I think a wait is a good idea. Seven days is not going to make any difference for anybody who needs a gun" (Alviani & Drake, 1983).

# NOTES

1    Up to $299 per such firearm transaction.

2    The basic approach to and shape of CGA 68, however, had been worked out by the Treasury Department in 1965.

3    Interstate transfers between federally licensed dealers were authorized under the Act.

4    Persons under 21 cannot purchase a handgun; those under 18 cannot purchase a long gun.

5    The Bureau's criminal enforcement function consumes most of its time and resources and is delegated to special agents with arrest power. This area deals with a broad spectrum of illegal firearms matters, such as illegal possession and trafficking, tracing crime guns, and conducting investigations in connection with criminal prosecutions.

6    Except to the extent of proscribing them from transferring weapons to anyone they knew or had reason to believe was a nonresident or otherwise ineligible to own firearms, a proscription virtually impossible to enforce in the private sector.

7    Hinckley was arrested in Nashville in October 1980 for carrying three guns, which the authorities confiscated. Four days later he purchased two .22 caliber revolvers, one of which was used to assault Reagan on March 30, 1981.

8    For example, the NRA had "roving patrols" of police officers fan out through the Capitol corridors assuring members of Congress that street-level officers were dead-set against the amendment.

9    Even less, since the Brady Bill did not require that prospective handgun buyers must be certified in gun proficiency or firearms safety before being allowed to take possession of a handgun.

# 4

# Polar Approaches to Crime Control

## MORTON GROVE HANDGUN BAN

Within a year after President Reagan was wounded by a handgun, there was a flurry of new gun control activity at the state and local levels throughout the country. Much of the renewed interest in gun control came from the action taken in Morton Grove, (Ill.), a suburb of Chicago with a population of 27,000. Determined to reduce handgun-related accidents and handgun crime, in June 1981 Morton Grove became the first locality in the nation to ban[1] the sale and possession of all handguns (*Sample Firearms Regulations in Illinois Municipalities,* 1983:13; *Newsweek,* 1982). Since Morton Grove enacted its controversial measure, upheld in several court challenges, some 400 towns and cities have started to press for similar ordinances (*Sample Firearms Regulations in Illinois Municipalities,* 1983:16; Kaplan, 1984:xi-xiii). In 1984, Oak Park, a community of 55,000 bordering one of Chicago's highest crime districts, followed Morton Grove's lead by banning the private possession of pistols. Just how seriously the ordinance was taken by Oak Park officials is illustrated by the Donald Bennett case. Donald Bennett was prosecuted for using his pistol to shoot at two robbers who had just taken $1200 in cash and jewelry from his gas station in an early morning holdup. It took a Cook County jury only 90 minutes to acquit Bennett of violating the town pistol ban. Bennett characterized his prosecution as a misapplication of the law, but the 30,000 member Illinois Council Against Handgun Violence lamented the above-the-law outcome in the case: "I hate to see anybody swayed by the argument that if you have a handgun you can somehow heroically help the police," said the group's chairman Rebecca Janowitz (*New York Times,* 1986d).

*Kennesaw's revenge.* In Kennesaw (Ga.), a town of 7,000 located near Atlanta, village officials were so incensed by the Morton Grove handgun ban that they passed an ordinance in 1982 which *required* all household heads[2] to keep a working firearm and supply of ammunition in their homes at all times. By doing so, Kennesaw gained instant fame as the only place

31

in the nation to formally adopt a policy of mandatory gun possession! Though at polar extremes, the Morton Grove and Kennesaw ordinances actually have much in common. The preambles to each (see Exhibit A) justify the action taken in the name of public welfare and as a deterrent to crime. Both towns claimed that serious crime dropped markedly since their new regulations went into effect, although there wasn't much serious crime in either place before then (*New York Times,* 1987a; *USA Today,* 1985). And both ordinances were largely symbolic, as evidenced by the *Bennett* case and by the comments of Kennesaw mayor Stephenson, who concedes that the mandatory ordinance is unenforceable. "We're not interested in searching people's houses. Mostly, what we wanted to do was make a statement, to make people sit up and take notice." It was also superfluous because about 90 percent of the Kennesaw population already owned guns before the law was passed. To underscore their contempt for handgun bans, in 1986 Kennesaw gave Donald Bennett a bronze plaque and key to the city and made him an honored guest at their 1987 "Freedom Day" rally commemorating passage of the village's one-of-a-kind gun law (*New York Times,* 1987a).

---

**Exhibit 4A**

*Thou Shalt Not Possess Handguns*

In order to protect and promote the health and safety and welfare of the public, no person in the Village of Morton Grove shall possess any handgun, unless the same has been rendered permanently inoperable.

—Morton Grove handgun ban ordinance

*Thou Shalt Bear Arms*

In order to provide for and protect the safety, security and general welfare of the city and its inhabitants, every head of household residing in the city limits is required to maintain a firearm together with ammunition therefore.

—Kennesaw mandatory gun ownership ordinance

---

# FLORIDA OPENS DOOR TO CONCEALED HANDGUNS

In 1987 Florida became the largest urbanized state to pass a law allowing almost any law-abiding citizen to carry a concealed handgun in public.[3] The controversial measure was spurred by an increase in violent crime (in a state already the national leader in this area), by a populace fed-up with being passive victims, and by the gun lobby's contention that "only an armed citizenry can stem the tide of crime" (*New York Times*, 1987d). As originally passed, the new law inadvertently erased the 1893 ban against the *un*concealed carrying of sidearms, making it legal to carry handguns in plain view (*USA Today*, 1987c). Officials quickly realized that the "Dodge City" image of citizens walking down the street or shopping in malls with handguns strapped to their hip could be disasterous for local business and the state's lucrative tourist industry. The legislature rectified the oversight by prohibiting the carrying of handguns in the open (*New York Times*, 1988a; *Time*, 1987b).

*State preemption.* When Governor Bob Martinez signed the measure, he wiped out some 400 local gun control laws by virtue of the doctrine of *state preemption,* under which the state's gun law supercedes all local gun control ordinances. The new "concealed-handgun" law therefore replaced the prior decentralized system of county control of gun regulations, which were invariably much stricter. For example, Broward County's rigorous gun law included a 10-day cooling-off period, an extensive police background investigation, a psychological examination, and having an "approved reason" (special-need) for wanting to carry a concealed handgun. Because of these stringent criteria—voided under state preemption—the county had issued only 24 licenses for concealed weapons (Murray, 1975:81; *New York Times*, 1987c; *Time*, 1987a). There is no longer any basis for denying a concealed handgun permit to anyone who meets the modest requirements listed in the act. Even felons and those with violent crime histories can qualify for a concealed-weapons permit because cases that are not "formally adjudicated" by a court or jury verdict are not part of the computer search for a prior criminal record. The law was also a savored victory for the NRA drive to urge state preemption as the means for abolishing municipal gun ordinances blocking handgun availability. The spectre of Morton Grove caused the NRA to campaign for preemption laws in 17 states, with Texas as its next preemption battle ground (*U.S. News & World Report*, 1987c; *New York Times*, 1987d).

*Citizens' enthusiastic response.* The ink on the legislation was hardly dry when officials were deluged with 36,000 applications for concealed weapons permits. And with 1,500 new requests a day, the figure was expected to soar to 150,000-200,000 in the first year alone (*New York Times*, 1987d; *U.S. News & World Report*, 1987c; *Time*, 1987a). Of the 26,086 people who applied for permits by February 1988, only 20 were turned down (*New York Times*, 1988b). Before state preemption, about 17,000 Floridians statewide were issued concealed-weapon permits, with over half the requests coming from three southern counties with restrictive regulation of concealed weapons (*USA Today,* 1987b). Dade County for example, which had the highest violent crime rate in the country, used to issue about 1,300 concealed weapons licenses a year; it now issues about 10,000 with the demand for permits continuing to boom (*Guns, Guns, Guns,* 1988). As a result of the law's safety-course requirement for a permit, citizens flocked to sign up for firearms classes offered by gun shops and at shooting ranges that started popping up all over the state. Two weeks after a brawny youth burst through her screen door, grabbed her purse and escaped to a waiting car, the shaken housewife was at a local shooting range aiming her new Smith & Wesson .38 Special at the silhouette of an assassin. "The robbery made me very paranoid, and I just want to protect myself. Next time I won't be afraid to use my gun" (*Time,* 1987a). The law itself did not require that would-be permit holders demonstrate proficiency in firearms use or shooting skills, only that applicants receive a signed certificate confirming that they took a gun-safety program (*USA Today,* 1987b; *New York Times,* 1987c).

*Caveat criminalis.* Legalizing access to concealed handguns struck a deep and widespread responsive chord among Florida's fear-ridden residents and merchants. The thinking behind the permissive handgun law was that "criminals already have guns. The police can't protect you [so] you've got to protect yourself" (*New York Times,* 1987c). Many citizens, like Bruce Lyon who was mugged in 1983, could readily identify with this position: "The law's just great. If muggers see you have a gun, they won't come" (*USA Today,* 1987c). It was contended that the law would thwart crime because criminals, at long last, would have reason to fear law-abiding citizens.

Not everyone was so sure about that. Critics maintained that the law would, quite literally, backfire when criminals wrested handguns from victims trying to defend themselves during a struggle. There was also concern that too many people authorized to carry a concealed handgun "are just dying for an opportunity to use it" (*U.S. News & World Report,* 1987b). Urban police chiefs were adamantly opposed to the proposal, and many local officers were plain scared about having to confront thousands of covertly armed individuals and the heightened danger attached to making routine traffic stops (*New York Times,* 1987d,1988a). "Before, when a policeman stopped a driver, the question was who had a gun. Today, the question is, who doesn't have a gun" (*USA Today,* 1987c). That remark may have been prophetic: after the third police officer in 30 days was shot during a routine traffic stop, the lawmakers were considering an amendment to let the voters decide whether to impose a seven-day cooling-off period for handgun sales (*USA Today,* 1988a). University of Miami criminologist Geoffrey Alpert predicted that the easy-access law would create "a new strata of gun owners—people who wouldn't have bought them if they had been forced to wait." Even those taking advantage of the law, like a computer repairman, had some reservations about it: "I'm just afraid of all the wackos out there [who will get handguns]" (*Time*, 1987a). It remains to be seen whether Florida's concealed handgun experiment will "scare off the thugs" or, instead, will lead to more innocent victims being shot (see Case-In-Point) and "make gunfire a frightening everyday phenomenon" (*U.S. News & World Report*, 1987c).

---

**Case-In-Point**

Arthur Kane, a distraught investor who lost $8.2 million in the October 1987 stock market crash, looked at a gun in the Timiami Gun Shop on Friday, filled out an application, and took possession of the weapon on Monday. An hour later he used the .357 calibre Magnum to murder one Merrill Lynch stockbroker, to shoot another who was left para-lyzed, and to commit suicide. Critics blamed Florida's new gun law, saying that "if the old law had been in effect [in Dade County where the incident occurred], maybe two people would be alive" (*USA Today*, October 29, 1987, p. 3A). Kane wasn't entitled to purchase any firearm because he had a felony conviction and had served six months on federal fraud charges, which he apparently concealed on the application form. While not admitting responsibility, the gun shop agreed to a settlement paying nearly $500,000 to the paralyzed victim and estate of the murder victim. Opponents of Florida's state preemption law launched a petition drive in July 1988 to extend the waiting period for handgun purchases from 48 hours, the interval when the law took effect, to seven days, the waiting period advocated in the Brady Bill (*USA Today*, July 15, 1988, p. 3A).

---

## MARYLAND BANS SATURDAY NIGHT SPECIALS

In 1988 Maryland passed a law banning the manufacture and sales of Saturday Night Specials, handing the NRA its worst defeat in years. In doing so, Maryland became the first state to outlaw a particular category of handguns deemed to have no socially useful or legitimate purpose. Not even a $5 million NRA campaign could prevail over Governor Schaefer's strong commitment to the measure, Handgun Control's ($100,000) lobbying effort, and a united front presented by the bill's proponents (*Washington Report*, 1988). The catalyst for the law was an increase in drug-related violence and a 1985 court decision which prevented SNS-crime victims from suing the gun manufacturer or the seller (*New York Times*, 1988c; *Time*, 1988c). (The bill also provided for the banning of plastic guns, which cannot be spotted by metal detectors.)

*Role of board.* The law established a special commission or board to decide, by the time it goes into effect in 1990, which handguns should be banned and to prepare a list of them. This nine-member board, appointed by the governor, will consist of private citizens, law enforcement officials, and gun lobby representatives. Handguns which the panel determines are easily concealable, poorly constructed and too inaccurate for sporting activities or self-defense will be placed on the prohibited list of illegal handguns (*New York Times,* 1988c). Maryland's unique approach resolved the problem of trying to legislatively define "SNSs" by allocating the task to a diversified panel with a vested interest and expertise in the area. After January 1990, manufacturers can be fined up to $10,000 and gun dealers up to $2500 for *each* banned handgun made or sold.

*NRA repeal effort fails.* No sooner had the governor signed the bill than the NRA moved swiftly to repeal the measure in a statewide referendum held in November 1988 (*New York Times,* 1988b). Since "SNSs" are not mentioned in the act and their definition is left up to the board's discretion, opponents claimed that the law could be applied to almost any type of handgun (*USA Today,* 1988b,f). The NRA launched an expensive TV blitz and canvassed urban neighborhoods door-to-door, telling residents that cheap handguns are often the only means the poor have for self-protection (*Time,* 1988c). But this time it was to no avail because Maryland residents voted overwhelmingly to retain the SNS ban (*New York Times,* 1988d). Liberals hoped that the Maryland initiative would have a domino effect and demonstrate that such reform measures could succeed despite NRA's Goliath spending power. Maryland's success could prove helpful to New Jersey, where State Senate President John Russo wants all handguns banned (*Time,* 1988a). Within days after the Maryland referendum, City Council members in Cincinnati voted to impose a 15-day waiting period for handgun buyers (*USA Today,* 1988e).

# NOTES

1   Like similar so-called "total bans," the ordinance identified several categories of people who were exempted from the ban, e.g., police, security guards, antique gun collectors, etc.

2   Unless lame or mentally impaired.

3   As well as other concealed firearms, knives, clubs, and tear gas guns. Concealed weapons could not be carried into certain designated areas, such as bars, courtrooms, police stations, polling places, and the State Legislature.

# 5

# Do Gun Control Laws Reduce Crime?

## FOREIGN COUNTRY COMPARISONS

Gun controllers make much of the fact that several foreign countries with tough firearms laws have much lower violent crime and murder rates than the United States. The handgun murder and violent crime rates in England and Japan where, respectively, even the bobbies are disarmed[1] and it is almost impossible for a private citizen to obtain a handgun, are miniscule by American standards (Bruce-Briggs, 1976:55-56; Harris, 1976:54). Comparisons with other European countries having similarly restrictive gun policies reveal that they too have relatively small amounts of violent crime, e.g., handgun homicides are 3.5 to 10 times greater in the United States (Danto, 1982:210; Kaplan, 1979:3).

The pitfalls in drawing any valid conclusions from such simple international comparisons is that they are compounded by vast cultural, political, economic and national character differences which may just as easily account for the differences in violent crime rates. An in-depth study of England's 1920 handgun ban by Cambridge University concluded that the law had no ascertainable effect on violent crime and that cultural factors were responsible for its comparative absence of violent crime (Kleck et al., 1982:14). England's aversion to personal violence is attributable to the population's docile character and deferential attitude toward authority, rather than to its rigorous gun control law (Kates, 1976a:30). Their rates of firearm ownership and violent crime were both very low for decades *before* England passed its strict new gun law, which has not prevented a sharp increase in gun crime there in the 1980s (Wright, 1988:32-33)! Japan's low crime rate can be explained by the widespread respect for law and order so deeply ingrained in the Japanese psyche, a cultural factor which also explains why Japanese-Americans (who have access to firearms here) have an even lower homicide rate than their gunless counterparts in Japan (*Ten Myths About Gun Control*, 1987:10; Kleck et al., 1982:15; Bruce-Briggs, 1976:55-56). The foreign-country argument for gun control effectiveness is further diminished by noting that free nations like Israel, Canada and

Switzerland have a heavily armed citizenry *and* much lower crime, murder, and suicide rates (see Close-up 5.1) than the United States (Bruce-Briggs, 1976:57; Kleck et al., 1982:16-17; Danto, 1982:210). Moreover, the implementation of foreign-style gun control sometimes involves highly intrusive ("unconstitutional") search and seizure procedures, greatly expanded police powers, confiscating legally obtained weapons, and little regard for the right to privacy—conditions which would probably not be tolerated in America for the sake of "gun control" (*Ten Myths About Gun Control,* 1987:10).

---

**CLOSE-UP 5.1: FIREARMS AND SUICIDE**

Guns account for just over one-half (58%) of the 30,000 suicides committed annually in the United States. The firearm-suicide rate has increased substantially among adolescents and young adults since 1970; an estimated 3,000 children a year use weapons to commit suicide (*Guns, Guns, Guns,* 1988:13; *The Banner,* 1987:1). Loaded handguns left around the house in the summer pose a special source of danger to depressed teenagers who are left unsupervised, are contemplating doing away with themselves, or who act out of impulse (Center to Prevent Handgun Violence News Release).

In a study of all suicides in Sacramento county during 1983-1985, Wintemute found that two-fifths were committed with handguns. Although handguns represented just 35 percent of firearms kept in the home, they were the overwhelming choice for committing suicide there: handguns were used in 70 percent of the firearm suicides committed at home and were the weapon of choice regardless of age or gender. "Many people who attempt suicide do so on impulse. So they look for an easily available means, which is often a handgun. Firearms—particularly handguns—are uniquely capable of translating such impulses into tragedy." The over-reliance on handgun suicide was attributed to their being kept loaded and within easy reach, and their short barrel making it easier to turn the weapon on oneself while pulling the trigger (Wintemute et al., 1988:825).

Lester and Murrell examined whether the strictness of state handgun control statutes had any effect in preventing suicides by firearms in 1960 and 1970. They found that states with stricter gun control laws had lower firearm suicide rates in both years. But they also had higher rates of suicide by other means, suggesting that reduced availability of one means of self-destruction may prompt suicide-prone individuals simply to utilize another means to do the job. The findings of an earlier study by the same authors, however, provide some support that handgun controls make impulsive suicide less likely (Lester and Murrell, 1982:131-139).

In their report to the Eisenhower Commission, Newton and Zimring (1969) came to the conclusion that "cultural factors appear to affect the suicide rates far more than the availability and use of firearms. Thus, suicide rates would not seem to be readily affected by making firearms less available." That conclusion was based on 1967 data in which the United States ranked ninth among a list of 16 nations, almost all of whom had more stringent firearms laws and much less per capita firearms ownership. The private stock of U.S. handguns increased from an estimated 27 million in 1967 to 41 million in 1975; yet in 1975 the U.S. suicide rate *dropped* to fifteenth among the listed countries (Kleck et al., 1982:38-39). After reviewing several American and foreign suicide studies, psychiatrist Bruce Danto concluded that "data show that people will find a way to commit suicide regardless of the availability of firearms" (Kleck et al., 1982:38-39; Danto, 1982:214). International comparisons also bode ill for preventing suicides through gun control. Several countries with stringent gun control have higher suicide rates than ours, or their people are noted for relying on other methods (poison, hanging) to commit suicide (Danto, 1982:214). Since Canada passed its strict gun control law in 1978, the U.S. suicide rate has been moving on a downward trend while Canada's suicide rate has been rising (Blackman, 1988).

## THE EFFECTIVENESS OF GUN CONTROL LAWS

Research findings on the effectiveness of gun control legislation are inconsistent, contradictory and inconclusive at best, with each side—too often having its own axe to grind—criticizing the other's methodology, research design and conclusions (Kessler, 1980:133). As a consequence, there is little consensus on the effects of the laws in general or of handgun restrictions in particular (McClain, 1984:214).

Using simple correlations between level of firearms ownership and the rate of gun use in crimes of violence, Newton and Zimring claim that more guns in private hands means more violence in society (Kleck, 1984b:102; Magaddino & Medoff, 1984:226). After comparing gun-related crime rates in two restrictive cities (New York, Chicago) with two permissive cities (Dallas, Phoenix), the President's Crime Commission similarly concluded that strong gun control laws are an effective means for controlling violent crime (Bendis & Balkin, 1979:439; Magaddino & Medoff, 1984:227). Such studies, however, have been faulted for not controlling other variables that might be more casually related to illegal gun use than firearms availability (Clark, 1984:9-10). Other studies have found no significant relationship between severity of gun regulations (or level of gun ownership) and violent crime rates (McClain, 1984:213; Kleck, 1986b:37, Riley, 1974:502; Blackman, 1985:34-35). Separate studies of the impact of the GCA 68 by Magaddino & Medoff, and Zimring found that the federal legislation did little to stem the amount of handgun violence or homicide, which led Zimring to back away from his earlier position on the efficacy of handgun controls (Magaddino & Medoff, 1984:226; Blackman, 1985:34-35). Five years after New Jersey's tough gun control law was passed in 1966, the state's murder rate increased by two-thirds, rape by 56 percent, and robbery soared 245 percent. The same upward trend occurred in Hawaii after it strengthened its gun regulations and banned SNSs (*Justice Reporter,* 1981:6).

Geisel et al. employed a rigorous methodology and multiple regression to measure the effectiveness of gun control legislation in the 50 states and in 129 cities. After controlling for ten socioeconomic characteristics and applying a "firearm control index" to measure each state's gun law require-ments, the researchers concluded that strong handgun control laws have a significant impact on reducing some types of violent crime (Geisel et al., 1969:670; McClain, 1984:211-212; Bendis & Balkin, 1979:439). They maintain that if the type of gun control legislation then existing in New Jersey were applied nationally, it would prevent 4,200-6,400 gun deaths a year (Riley, 1974:503). But University of Wisconsin economist Douglas Murray disputed their findings in a subsequent study based on census data from the 50 states. Taking into account a number of social variables in focusing on seven types of handgun laws (ranging from purchase permits to waiting periods), Murray examined the interstate variation in murder, rob-bery, assault and accidental firearm death rates (*Justice Reporter,* 1981:6). "On the basis of these data, the conclusion is, inevitably, that gun control laws [or the relative availability of handguns] have no individual or collec-tive effect in reducing the rates of violent crime" (Murray, 1975:88; *Justice Reporter,* 1981:6). It is questionable, though, whether Murray's conclusion can be taken at face value because his results may be affected by the leak-age phenomenon. "As long as there is no national gun control law [with teeth in it] and there are states in which the purchase of firearms is virtu-ally unencumbered, state-by-state comparisons such as that employed by the Wisconsin study are of little value" (Drinan, 1976:52).

If it is incumbent upon those urging stricter gun control measures to prove that restrictive laws work, then there is a glaring lack of evidence that the kinds of control laws proposed or tried have been notably or even marginally efficacious (Kates, 1976a:32). If tough gun control laws are for naught, the main reasons for their inability to impact violent crime are to be found in how criminals acquire firearms, their commitment to a lifestyle involving violence, the nature of domestic homicide and the "sub-stitution" issue.

## NOTES

1   Although the English patrol force is disarmed, a large contingent of armed rov-ing detectives are quickly available to distribute weapons to bobbies in immi-nent danger and to use fatal force when necessary.

# 6

# Obstacles to Gun Control

## CRIMINAL ACQUISITION OF FIREARMS

The most comprehensive information on the parameters of firearms and related matters among serious offenders comes from the Wright-Rossi study (the Felon Survey) based on self-administered questionnaires to 1,874 incarcerated felons in 10 states in 1982. The findings are even more significant because they support the position long espoused by the NRA—if what the inmates said in the questionnaires is true—and because the senior author is a nationally recognized scholar who, before undertaking the investigation, took for granted the desirability of gun control. The Felon Survey analysis subdivided the entire sample into seven categories of criminals based on whether guns were ever used in committing crimes and the frequency of such gun use (see Table 6.1). The "handgun predator" group is of special interest because it consists of offenders who had committed numerous gun crimes and because contemporary gun control efforts are geared toward handgun control of one kind or another.

*Private transfers.* Only 1 out of 6 handgun owners obtained their most-recent handgun through customary retail transactions from a licensed dealer (Wright and Rossi, 1986:185). The rest obtained them through off-the-record private transfers involving friends (the most common method), relatives, acquaintances, off-the-street purchases, from the grey market and by theft. A sizeable portion of all informal private transfers were of questionable legality in that the law forbids private parties from knowingly transferring a firearm to a convicted felon. Yet many acquaintances apparently sold, gave or traded guns to known criminals with seeming indifference to the law, recognizing that there was little chance of their being caught or punished (Wright & Rossi, 1986:191). One of the questions indicated the ease with which the men felt they could arm themselves upon release from prison and the irrelevance of gun laws in thwarting their access to firearms. Most of the gun owners and nonowners alike thought

**Table 6.1 Felon Survey Typology of Offenders**

| Criminal Type | Number of offenders | Percent of total sample | Total criminality score[†] |
|---|---|---|---|
| *Total Sample* | 1,874 | 100 | 139 |
| Unarmed criminals | 725 | 39 | 61 |
| Armed not-with-a-gun criminals | | | |
| improvisors | 79 | 4 | 101 |
| knife criminals | 134 | 7 | 109 |
| Gun criminals | | | |
| one-time gun users | 257 | 14 | 84 |
| sporadic gun users | 257 | 14 | 151 |
| handgun predators | 321 | 17 | 332 |
| shotgun predators | 101 | 5 | 265 |

Source: James D. Wright, "The Armed Criminal in America," *Research in Brief,* National Institute of Justice, November 1986, p. 2.

[†]"Total criminality" is an index measure or score reflecting the sum of all the crimes that the felon had ever committed (as reported in the study questionnaire) weighted by the seriousness of each offense. The index numbers have no intrinsic meaning except that lower numbers mean fewer or less serious crimes and higher numbers mean more frequent or more serious ones. The table shows the average score on this index for each group.

that it would be "no trouble at all" to obtain a gun upon release; and about 80 percent felt that they could get a suitable handgun *in a few days* from friends, on the street or from illicit contacts. The typical gun-owning felon expected to have no difficulty getting a weapon almost immediately (one day) after release. The above findings suggest that gun restrictions which attempt to prevent criminals' firearm acquisition via licensed retail sales (as most laws do) may be doomed to failure. This is because the hardcore criminal element relies on alternative sources of supply which have low visibility, with which the official system is not equipped to deal, and which are hard to regulate or cannot be regulated.

*Gun theft.* Gun theft played a surprisingly important role in the criminals' acquisition of firearms: almost half (47%) of the total sample reported that they had ever stolen any firearm during their criminal careers. Among the handgun owners, one-third had personally stolen their most recent handgun; and if the handguns stolen by someone else before winding up in the inmates' hands are included, then 70 percent of their most recent handguns were probably stolen weapons. Moreover, there was an ominous tendency for the highest levels of gun theft to be concentrated among the criminal groups who most often use guns to commit crime. For example, 81 percent of the handgun predators admitted to stealing at least one gun, and the average number of guns stolen per handgun predator was 47 (Wright &

Rossi, 1986:196-198)! Gun theft was basically a crime of opportunity by offenders who were already gun owners: three-quarters of the gun thieves only stole firearms when they came across them while committing a burglary whose principle target was other items (cameras, TVs) that could be disposed of readily and profitably. Nonetheless, fully two-thirds of the gun thieves and 90 percent of the handgun predators retained at least one of the stolen weapons for their own personal use. The heavy volume of gun theft from legitimate owners and private residences—estimated as high as half a million a year—and the infeasibility of confiscation makes this avenue of firearms availability an especially difficult one to contain (Drinan, 1976:49). What might prove useful are public education programs which alert citizens to the gun theft problem and provide specific procedures and technology for making their firearms more theft-proof (Wright & Rossi, 1986).

## CRIMINALS' FIREARMS PREFERENCES

Some gun control policies and proposals have targeted SNSs on the grounds that legitimate gun owners have no need or interest in such firearms while criminals most decidedly do, as revealed by confiscation studies. However, based on the felons' stated preferences about the characteristics they look for in a suitable ("ideal") handgun *and* the kind of handguns the felons actually carried, the emphasis on removing SNSs from the firearms market may be misplaced or have little impact on the serious offender.

*Most-recent handgun traits.* The assumed criminal preference for cheap, short barrel SNS-type handguns was not confirmed in the Felon Survey. On the contrary, the felons' preference was for accurate, well-made, large caliber weapons rather than the characteristics associated with SNSs (Wright & Rossi, 1986:15). Their stated preferences were borne out by the handguns the felons actually carried. Their most recent handguns were, on the average, relatively expensive (two-thirds worth over $100), 70 percent had barrel lengths 4 inches or over, and the same proportion were large (over .32)[1] caliber handguns (Wright & Rossi, 1986:170-171). The most common recent handgun was a Smith & Wesson .38 revolver with a 4-inch barrel, the sidearm of issue in about 90 percent of all police departments; and a considerable number (almost one-fifth) were the large "Dirty Harry" type handguns with 7-inch or longer barrel lengths (Lester Murrell, 1982:131-139). No more than 15 percent of the recent handguns would qualify as SNSs under the standard definition of the term (Wright, 1986:3). The preference for SNS-style handguns was concentrated among felons who never owned a gun and never committed a gun crime (Wright & Rossi: 1986:166-167). The preference for and possession of heavy-duty handguns was strongest in the more predatory felon typologies, so that "the strategy of purging the market of small, cheap handguns [SNSs] may be largely irrelevant to the felons most likely to commit gun crimes" (Wright & Rossi, 1986:15).

## SUBSTITUTION

If there were a completely effective ban against and confiscation of *all handguns*, would individuals who previously used handguns to commit crime or settle arguments switch to less lethal weapons like knives (or go unarmed), or would they substitute long guns in their stead? The "substitution" issue is an argument over whether offenders unable to obtain handguns would substitute less dangerous or more dangerous weapons. If all types of firearms (including long guns) were eliminated, would-be assailants would have no choice but to rely on less dangerous weapons and substitution would necessarily be beneficial (Kleck et al., 1982:33). However, because public sentiment is so overwhelmingly opposed to placing restrictions on rifles and shotguns, gun control proposals leave most long guns untouched and available as replacements (substitutes) for banned handguns (Kaplan, 1984:13).

Gun controllers claim that there would be very little long gun substitution because their non-concealability makes them unsuitable for most gun crimes; and handguns are uniquely criminogenic in crime-of-passion and altercation killings. If so, the outcome of handgun-prohibition would be a reduction in gun violence and far fewer homicides (Kleck, 1986b:48; Kates, 1979:112). Gun proponents counter that rather than "going straight," criminals who previously used handguns will simply resort to sawed-off long guns to achieve the same result and that unmodified long guns can just as conveniently be used to "settle arguments" which occur within the home (Jacobs, 1986:13).

*Single-minded vs. ambiguous intent.* The criminological focal point for applying substitution theory is how the homicide picture would be affected if handguns were unavailable. To the extent that homicide is the result and expression of a *single-minded* intention to kill or inflict grievous injuries, then long gun substitution would be quite common. This is the position taken by Marvin Wolfgang in his classic study *Patterns of Criminal Homicide:* "It is the contention of this observer that few homicides due to shooting could be avoided merely if a firearm were not immediately present, [because] the offender would select some other weapon to achieve the same destructive goal, "i.e., there is more than one way to skin a cat (Wolfgang, 1958:83; Riley, 1974:504). According to this perspective, homicide offenders are so highly motivated (determined) toward fatal aggression or bent to venting their anger or frustration that nothing will stand in their way—including the absence of a handgun.

On the other hand, gun controllers adhere to the opposite view, espoused by Zimring, that the mindset of most homicide offenders is *ambiguous* (flexible) and thus subject to change, depending upon circumstances in their immediate environment. In particular, in crimes of passion and other non-stranger killings, the offenders allegedly do not set out to inflict grievous harm or destroy their victims. They may not even be fully aware of the consequences of their actions, so that "the more ambiguous intention might well lead to the termination of an attack before lethal consequences ensue" were handguns not so readily accessible (Riley, 1974:504).

*Determinants of homicide.* In a handgun-free society, there would actually be a combination of weapon substitutions, with some prospective killers switching to knives (or foregoing crime) and others shifting to shotguns and rifles. Whether homicide would increase or decrease under handgun-abolition depends on two variables: the proportion of assailants accustomed to using handguns who would substitute long guns, and how much more deadly long guns are compared to handguns. If a handgun ban caused 30 percent of such assailants to switch to long guns (Zimring's figure), then the number of firearm homicides would double. And if the magnitude of long gun substitution were closer to 50-75 percent (as Kleck estimates) then the amount of homicide would triple or quadruple (Kleck, et al., 1982:33-34; Kates, 1979). The reason that an apparently modest shift to long guns (like 30%) would produce a net increase in homicide is that "at a minimum, a shot fired from a long gun is four times[2] as likely to kill as one fired from a handgun" (Kates, 1979:111; Kleck, 1986b:49). Thus, gun control efforts could turn out to be a "policy disaster" in the making (Kleck et al., 1982:33). For even if these handgun-prohibition policies "were effective in reducing handgun possession [among criminals], they would almost certainly have the perverse effect of causing more people to die than would have died without the measure" (Kleck, 1986b:50).

*Substitution "from the horses' mouth."* Perhaps the best source for shedding light on the substitution factor is the Felon Survey inmates themselves. Sixty-four percent believed that if deprived of handguns, criminals would start carrying sawed-off long guns; only one-fifth predicted the criminal element would switch to knives or clubs. As for the felons' *personal* substitution choices, two-fifths[3] of the entire sample said they would upgrade their weaponry to sawed-off long guns, while one-quarter would substitute less lethal weapons. And if they could not indulge their preferences for SNSs because of a SNS-only ban, almost half said they would carry larger caliber, more expensive handguns.

The most significant and alarming finding is that the handgun predator group—those most likely to commit handgun crime and the most vicious assaults—were the ones most inclined to substitute more dangerous weaponry: if deprived of desired SNSs, 85 percent would carry larger caliber handguns (68%) or sawed-off shoulder weapons (18%). And in the face of a total handgun ban, 72 percent of the handgun predators, and half of the sporadic gun users, would respond by carrying sawed-off long guns (Wright & Rossi, 1986:216-217). "The general pattern is thus one of lateral or upward substitution . . . The message these men seem to be sending is that their felonious activities would not suffer for lack of appropriate armament" (Wright, 1986:5). Wright emphasizes that the felons' substitution statements are accurate reflections of what they would actually do under the specified restrictive gun control policies. This is because half of all men in the sample, and 77 percent of the handgun predators, who *said* they would substitute sawed-off weapons if confronted with a total handgun ban *had* sawed-off a rifle or shotgun at some time in their lives and felt it would be "very easy" for them to do so again (Wright & Rossi, 1986:220). The implications of these findings are that, at least among serious adult felons, the likely response to banning SNSs or all handguns would be a net substitution shift toward *more* rather than less lethal equipment with disasterous consequences for society (Wright & Rossi, 1986:223).

## HOMICIDE BY "ORDINARY CITIZENS"

An important aspect of the argument for some type of handgun prohibition is that it will reduce homicides by disarming individuals who use handguns to kill people they know (Kleck, 1986b:40). The rationale for this position runs along the following lines: "Homicide is largely a matter of domestic and acquaintance killings by ordinary citizens who happen to have a loaded handgun available to them in a moment of rage" (Kleck, et al., 1982:25). These crime-of-passion and altercation killings ("non-felony-related" homicides) are isolated outbursts of violence by individuals who are otherwise law abiding, not violence-prone, and have clean records. Precisely because they are law-abiding and not assaultive criminals by nature, ordinary citizens will comply with handgun restrictions, unlike hardened criminals who commit premeditated murder or kill someone in the course of perpetrating another felony like robbery (a "felony-related" homicide) (Kleck et al., 1982:25).

How valid are the assumptions underlying this profile of the ordinary-citizen homicide offender?

*Nonfelony-related homicides exaggerated.* Federal Bureau of Investigation (FBI) data reveal that in 1987 nearly 3 out of every 5 murder victims were related to (17%) or acquainted with (40%) their assailants, compared to 20 percent which occurred in connection with other felonious activities (*Crime in the United States,* 1987:11-12). It is these "non-felony-related" homicides by ordinary citizens which, theoretically, can be substantially reduced through handgun restrictions. However, many of the homicides classified by the FBI as nonfelony-related involve vicious assaults by street gang members against rivals, contract murder taken out on competitors, and, increasingly, drug disputes between acquaintances or business associates (*A Question of Self-Defense,* 1987). Although such killings are officially listed as nonfelony-related because the offender "knew" the victim beforehand, for all intents and purposes they are felony-related and probably cannot be prevented through the expediency of handgun controls (Rose & Deskins, 1986:90).

*The myth of the nonviolent murderer.* There is little basis for the belief that handguns are a catalyst to crimes of passion committed by normally placid, peaceful, subdued individuals—i.e., that "it's nice people who are killing each other" (Gettinger, 1980:10). Studies show that rather than being isolated incidents, the murder of a family member or acquaintance is "the culminating event in a long history of interpersonal violence between the parties" or part of a continuing pattern of generalized violent behavior (*A Question of Self-Defense,* 1987; Kleck, 1986b:41). The popular image of the model citizen who suddenly goes berserk and kills a loved one or friend is largely a media myth fostered by reporters who "play up" the dramatic contrast between extremely violent acts by persons with supposedly nothing in their background to indicate they were capable of such behavior (Kleck, 1986b:40). For example, news accounts of Texas Tower killer Charles Whitman invariably mentioned that Whitman had been a choir boy and an Eagle Scout. Conspicuously omitted or relegated to the back pages were that he was raised in a violent home, had been a chronic wife abuser, and was court-martialed in the Marines for fighting (Kleck, 1986b:40). "The apparently 'nonviolent' killer is a rare exception to a rather mundane general rule: People who are seriously violent in the present almost invariably have been seriously violent in the past" (Kleck, 1986b:40).

*Prior records of murderers.* Prior records of murderers indicate that a majority have prior arrest records and perhaps half of them have previous convictions (Kleck, 1984a:42). Moreover, the arrest records of acquaintance killers substantially underestimate their real history of assaultive behavior because their victims are less likely to press charges and the police are loathe to interfere in a family matter (Kleck et al., 1982:26). A study of police responding to domestic disturbance calls in Kansas City (Missouri) found that 90 percent of all the family homicides were preceded by previous disturbances at the same address, with a median of 5 calls per address. Thus, homicide—of a stranger or someone known to the offender— is "usually part of a pattern of violence, engaged in by people who are known to the police, and presumably others, as violence-prone" (Kleck, 1984a:43). As many as three-quarters of the domestic murderers have been previously arrested and about half previously convicted of crimes (Kleck, 1986b:40). Research confirms that the typical homicide offender has an extensive prior arrest record that includes at least one crime of violence. "In short, the average murderer turns out to be no less hardened a criminal than the average robber or burglar. There is, therefore, no more reason to think that he [or she] will cavil at violating a handgun ban than will they" (Kleck et al., 1982:26).

*Impulsive homicide and substitution.* The belief that handguns are especially dangerous in heat of passion killings and that long gun substitution would not occur is unfounded. This is because long guns are kept primarily in the home, where most fatal attacks between spouses and relatives take place; and citizens own twice as many long guns as handguns (Clark, 1984:21). "The circumstances in which homicides occur would easily permit long guns to be substituted in anywhere from 54 percent to about 80 percent of the cases" (Kleck, 1984c:195). A long gun, for example, can be kept in a closet, under the bed, or next to the door just as easily as a handgun can be kept in a bureau drawer (Kleck, 1984c:188). In homicides which occur within the home, "weapon concealability is irrelevant, and involve weapons that were obtained during the argument, not carried [on the person] before it" (Kates, 1979:112). That most nonstranger homicides stem from "spur of the moment" quarrels over sex, money, power, abuse or perceived challenges to masculinity does not necessarily mean that the offenders were armed at the time. Instead, a common scenario is that when the dispute reaches a "boiling point" which triggers unrestrained aggression, the killer goes to an adjacent bedroom or a nearby car to get a firearm (Kates, 1979:114). Long guns owned by and kept in the *victim's* home also can become accessible to the offender during an interpersonal conflict episode, because victims themselves are often the first ones to introduce a firearm into a tense situation (Kleck, 1984c:188-189).

# NOTES

1  Compared to only 47 percent of all handguns manufactured in the United States in 1973-1974 that were greater than .32 caliber.

2  The only way an effective handgun ban would probably *not* lead to an increase in homicide is if criminals substituted long guns that were only marginally more lethal than handguns, i.e., if criminals chose the least dangerous type of long gun in making the switch, which is highly unlikely.

3  A larger figure than the 30 percent estimate utilized above.

# 7

# Enforcement and Compliance with Handgun Ban

## PROHIBITION-ERA COMPARISON

Many authorities are convinced that any federal law imposing an outright ban on the sale and possession of all handguns would be unenforceable, encounter widespread noncompliance and be doomed to failure just as the "great experiment" in alcoholic prohibition was. "Why would we expect the outcome of 'handgun prohibition" to differ from its 1920s predecessor?" (Wright, 1988:23) Kates is concerned that:

> even partial enforcement of a handgun prohibition would result in large numbers of snoopers and informers, 'stop-and-frisk' laws, 'no-knock' searches, and other repugnant police practices. The result of such invasions of privacy would probably be the jailing of hundreds of thousands of otherwise law-abiding citizens who would react to gun prohibition with the same self-righteous spirit against tyranny that greeted liquor and marijuana prohibitions (Kates, 1976a:31).

Just as occurred during Prohibition, a black market dominated by organized crime would allegedly satisfy the public's unabated demand for the outlawed item and the police would be paid to look the other way (Clark, 1984:11; Kessler, 1980:141). The liquor laws were routinely ignored despite the fact that they were far more enforceable than gun control laws. Alcoholic beverages are rapidly consumed and need to be constantly re-supplied, which increased the chances of being caught violating the Volstead Act. By comparison, each presently owned gun stays in circulation indefinitely and, under a handgun ban, would be undetectable until it was used or the government took steps to recover them (Kleck et al., 1982:43).

## LAX ENFORCEMENT AND ILLEGAL SEARCHES

A persistent claim is that handgun-prohibition would do little good since the enforcement of the gun laws *presently* on the books is so lax, erratic, lenient and legally suspect (Kleck, 1986b:52). Minimal criminal justice resources are directed to detecting gun law violators. Arrests for illegal gun possession are usually made only incident to arrest on some other more serious, substantive charge, like robbery or burglary. Special projects like the one in Rochester (New York) which aggressively sought out gun violators and operated along the lines of tactical narcotic units, are few and far between (Gettinger, 1980:18).

When a gun registration law that also prohibited carrying a concealed weapon went into effect in Chicago in 1968, a study of cases from Cook County Circuit Court found "a pattern of low and steadily declining enforcement . . ." (Bendis & Balkin, 1979:442). A prominent reason for the low conviction rate in illegal gun possession cases is that many defendants are dismissed[1] because the weapons are discovered through illegal searches—the officer does not have "probable cause" for conducting the search (Bendis & Balkin, 1979:442). About one-third of Chicago's simple gun possession cases were dismissed on these grounds, as were almost 70 percent of all firearms charges by Michigan courts (Kessler, 1980:138-139). And in an unidentified large city, the police made 25,000 illegal searches (which produced 117 firearms) in recent years "on the theory that any black driving a late model car has an illegal gun" (Kates, 1976b:55).

*Lenient sentences.* When convictions are obtained for illegal gun possession, the standard disposition is probation or small fines rather than jail time. Therefore, "what good would stronger gun laws do when the courts have demonstrated that they will not enforce them?" (Kates, 1984:148-152). In the Chicago study mentioned above, the typical punishment was a fine of about $90; no more than 6 percent of those prosecuted under the law were sentenced to jail, for an average of 36 days (Bendis & Balkin, 1979:447; Kleck, 1986b:53). In part, police, prosecutors and courts give low priority to enforcement because law-abiding citizens whose only crime is illegal possession are not perceived as the "bad guys" (Kleck, 1986b:55).

## WIDESPREAD FLOUTING OF HANDGUN BAN?

Opponents of handgun-prohibition rest their case on the (seemingly contradictory[2]) contentions that a sizeable portion of the gun-owning public will disregard the law just as drinkers did during Prohibition, and that if guns are outlawed, only outlaws will have guns. "No matter what laws we enact, they will be obeyed only by the law-abiding. . . . Why should we expect felons to comply with a gun law when they readily violate laws against robbery, assault, and murder?" (Wright, 1988:30). The Prohibition analogy may be somewhat misleading though, because the Volstead Act applied to *all* alcoholic beverages; and whether the average citizen's desire to own handguns is as strong as the proclivity to imbibe is arguable. That enforcement of a handgun ban would be selective and incomplete may not be a sufficient basis for abandoning the idea, as few laws enjoy uniformly high compliance (Drinan, 1976:48).

*Compliance among self-protection owners.* Whether there would be large-scale defiance of a handgun ban depends mainly on the risk of detection for violating the law and the type of gun owner (Kleck et al., 1982:46). Compliance would probably be highest among sportsmen because of the high risk of being detected if they continued to use handguns for target shooting or hunting. The situation is different, however, for self-protection handgun owners, who keep guns out of perceived necessity rather than recreation, who would have strong incentives to flout the law, and whose risk of detection and punishment (even if caught) would be low (Kates, 1984:148-152).

Of course, people who think of themselves as law abiding usually obey laws they consider *legitimate* even if they do not like them or believe their chances of getting caught breaking the law are slight. But in the event of a complete handgun ban, rationalizations and rationales readily come to mind which undermine the perceived legitimacy of such a law: the belief that a government which cannot protect its citizens from crime has no right to stop them from trying to do so, that they have an inalienable right to keep and bear arms under the Second Amendment (see Close-up 7.1) and the examples of "opinion leaders who have preached for years against protection ownership turn out to be opposing it only for people who do not have the influence they [do] to get a protection gun for themselves" (Kates, 1984:155).

*Baltimore buy-back program.* In 1974 Baltimore experimented with a buy-back program that offered citizens $50 for each operable handgun turned in to the authorities and immunity from prosecution for illegal possession. Ironically, the program was discontinued after three months because it was too successful: the city ran out of funds after recovering 13,000 guns at a cost of $750,000 (Kaplan, 1981:19-20). In a related proposal that never got off the ground, a report to the governor of Massachusetts recommended offering bounties to individuals for notifying the authorities about friends or relatives who possessed guns illegally. Informers could remain anonymous or use code names or identification numbers. If the tip resulted in confiscation of the illegal weapon, the tipsters would be paid a specified "bounty" (Kates, 1984:162).

*Confiscation.* Short of confiscation, there may be no foreseeable conditions under which enough gun owners could be persuaded to give up their handguns in order for the ban to be workable (Kaplan, 1981:14). Confiscation, however, could only be implemented legally and conveniently on the street through currently recognized "stop and frisk" procedures which are directed toward suspected "real criminals" rather than self-protection handgun owners (Clark, 1984:17-19). Nor are the courts likely to authorize street-level (as opposed to airport) use of metal detectors by the police to detect who is carrying a concealed handgun (Kates, 1984:160-161). The only way to remove the main stockpile of handguns would be through a massive program of house-to-house searches. Any such action would be blatantly unconstitutional, offensive to the principles of an open society, would solidify public support for civil disobedience, pose a real danger to the "intruding" police officers making the searches, and require law enforcement personnel and expenditures[3] which are simply not available (Kaplan, 1981:14).

---

**CLOSE-UP 7.1: THE RIGHT TO BEAR ARMS**

A well regulated Militia, being necessary to the security of a free State, the right of the people to keep and bear Arms, shall not be infringed.

—Second Amendment

The NRA, Second Amendment Foundation and other opponents of gun control have long espoused that individuals have an unqualified right to own firearms which is ensconced in and protected by the Second Amendment (Bruce-Briggs, 1976:57). The meaning of the Second Amendment, however, is subject to conflicting interpretations. The main controversy is over whether the Second Amendment "acts only as a prohibition against federal interference with State militia"—thereby conferring a *collective* right to bear arms in the service of the state—or whether it guarantees citizens an *individual* right to keep and carry firearms as a private matter for their own self-protection (Marina, 1984:436). There is an extensive body of authority supporting the interpretation that the Second Amendment protects a collective right of the states to arm a militia for the common defense (Beard & Rand, 1987:13). "It's been upheld for decades that you do not have a Constitutional right to have bazookas and hand grenades. The only thing new legally is that the weapons being banned are guns" (*Newsweek*, 1982).

*Intent of framers.* The most serious grievance voiced by the colonists at the First Continental Congress in Philadelphia in 1776 was the oppressive conditions they were subjected to under British rule: martial law, the arbitrary exercise of power by the Crown's standing army, illegal searches without cause, being forced to feed and quarter British troops in their homes, etc. By the time of the American Revolution, through bitter experience, the colonists had developed a deep distrust of the concentration of power in the hands of a strong central government, which might once again become an instrument of tyranny and oppression (Spitzer, 1986:244; Bruce-Briggs, 1976:58). The primary concern of the founding fathers was to avoid a reoccurrence of the political and social abuses which spawned the Bill of Rights. The Second Amendment was therefore adopted to ensure the states' capacity to mount an effective military response against tyrannical federal actions (or foreign invaders) via local armed militia—the backbone of resistance to British oppression—should the need ever again arise (Spitzer, 1986:244). James Madison said as much in observing that "as the greatest danger to the liberty is from large standing armies, it is best to prevent them by an effectual provision of a good Militia." (Riley, 1974:516). Accordingly, "there was no intention of the Founding Fathers to guarantee the use of firearms for recreation, nor for self-defense against criminals," i.e., as a personal right (Bruce-Briggs, 1976:58).

*Gun supporters view of history.* Gun control detractors and more recent scholarship in the area have a somewhat different reading and emphasis of the historical record. According to the individual-right assessment, the common law heritage acknowledging the keeping of firearms for self-defense was transported lock, stock and barrel to America by colonists who never questioned that such a personal right existed at the time the Second Amendment was adopted (Caplan, 1982:793; Kluin, 1982:248; Kates, 1983:240). The personal right to keep arms may have been inextricably linked to a grass roots militia, "but the advocates of control of firearms should not argue that the Second Amendment did not intend for Americans of the late eighteenth century to possess arms for their own personal defense . . . " (Marina, 1984:438).

*Judicial construction.* The opinion of legal scholars and American case law support the collective view that the Amendment only restricts the federal government from infringing on the state's ability to maintain and arm a militia (Kluin, 1982:245-246; Spitzer, 1986:243-244). In its initial consideration of the issue, the Supreme Court ruled that the states are free to regulate firearms as they choose because the Second Amendment is not "incorporated" into the Fourteenth Amendment and, therefore, the Second Amendment is not applicable to the states (*United States v. Cruikshank,* 90 U.S 542 [1876]; *Presser v. Illinois,* 116 U.S. 252 [1886]; *Miller v. Texas,* 153 U.S. 535 [1894]). Because of its nonincorporation, all the Second Amendment can do is to invalidate certain gun control measures which the *federal* government might adopt (Alviani & Drake, 1983:9-10; Spitzer, 1986:243; Freiburn, 1982:1092).

The leading case in which the High Court dealt directly with the meaning of the Second Amendment was *United States v. Miller,* where the defendant was convicted of transporting an unregistered sawed-off shotgun across state lines in violation of the National Firearms Act of 1934.

In Miller, the Court affirmed the concept of a collective right and upheld the conviction because the defendant could not show how possession of a shotgun with a barrel of less than 18 inches bore a "reasonable relationship to the preservation or efficiency of a well regulated militia" (Riley, 1974:518; Spitzer, 1986:243-244). Hence, the Court "cannot say that the Second Amendment guarantees the right to keep and bear such an instrument" (*United States v. Miller,* 307 U.S. 174 [1939]). Utilizing the Court's "militia-related" criterion, a federal statue banning Saturday Night Specials presumably would not violate the Second Amendment, total confiscation of all firearms would; and the legality of prohibiting "assault type" rifles would depend on whether they were deemed suitable for "a well regulated militia" (Kaplan, 1984:xxvi).

"Every federal court decision that has considered the issue has given the Second Amendment a collective, militia interpretation," and no gun control measure has ever been declared unconstitutional on Second Amendment grounds (Beard & Rand, 1987:14). In upholding a Morton Grove (Ill.) ban on possessing handguns, the Seventh Circuit Court stated unequivocally "possession of handguns by individuals is not part of the right to keep and bear arms." The court indicated that such a ban was a valid exercise of the state's police power, so long as the ordinance bears a reasonable relationship to the protection of public health, safety, morals and the general welfare (Freiburn, 1982:1108). The Supreme Court refused to hear a challenge to the Morton Grove law in 1983, and in 1984 the Illinois Supreme Court upheld the ordinance (Beard & Rand, 1987:14).

## PUBLIC OPINION ON GUN CONTROL

Pollsters have been measuring public opinion on gun control since 1938, when the Gallup Poll asked: "Do you think all owners of pistols and revolvers should be required to register with the government?" (79% responded yes) (Shields, 1981:71). The standard gun-control question, first asked in the 1959 Gallup poll, was whether the public favored or opposed a law that would require people to obtain a police permit before buying a gun (see Table 7.1) In that and subsequent years, the proportion endorsing a police permit has been between 68-82 percent (Wright, 1981:31-32). "What these data suggest, in short, is that most people feel that the ownership and use of handguns should be taken at least as seriously by governments as the ownership and use of automobiles is" (Wright, 1981:32). It is well-documented that "the vast majority of Americans have favored *some kind of action* (emphasis added) for the control of civilian firearms" for a long time (Wright, 1981:31). Besides endorsing registration and police permits, for example, there is immense public support for waiting-periods and mandatory sentences for using guns to commit crime (Wright, 1981:34).

**Table 7.1 Survey of Public Opinion on Gun Control**

| Do you favor or oppose: | % Favor | Oppose | No Opinion |
|---|---|---|---|
| 1.  the registration of all handguns? | 70 | 25 | 6 |
| 2.  making the laws covering the sale of handguns more strict? | 60 | 38 | 2 |
| 3.  continuing the present federal law banning the sale of handguns in one state to a person or dealer from another state? | 67 | 23 | 10 |
| 4.  a law which would require a person to obtain a police permit before he or she could buy a gun? | 70 | 27 | 3 |
| 5.  cracking down on illegal sales? | 85 | 11 | 5 |
| 6.  instituting a waiting period before a handgun can be purchased to allow for a criminal records check? | 88 | 7 | 5 |
| 7.  required mandatory prison sentences for all persons using a gun in a crime? | 83 | 12 | 6 |
| 8.  banning the future manufacture and sale of non-sporting type handguns? | 48 | 41 | 11 |
| 9.  banning the future manufacture and sale of small, cheap, low quality handguns? | 70 | 23 | 7 |
| 10. using public funds to buy back and destroy existing handguns on a voluntary basis? | 33 | 56 | 11 |
| 11. using public funds to buy back and destroy existing handguns on a mandatory basis? | 28 | 62 | 12 |

Source: Questions 1-5 from *1987 Sourcebook of Criminal Justice Statistics,* Washington, DC: Bureau of Justice Statistics, 1988, pp. 172-174; questions 6-11 from *1980 Sourcebook.*

*Caveats on "public opinion."* The data from polls and surveys, however, are not indicative of unambiguous, "overwhelming" public support and demand for stricter gun control measures; in actuality, the public is divided regarding the kind of gun controls it wants and can live with (*New York Times,* 1981). "Public opinion" responses on this subject are highly sensitive to how the questions are phrased and presented, to how much "gun control" will cost, and to shocking incidents of mass killings by firearms (Wright, 1981:31). For example, an identical proportion of the public approve of police permits buy oppose "a law giving police the power to decide who may or may not own a firearm." A solid majority favor registration but oppose "the federal government's spending $4 billion to enact a gun registration program" or using public funds for buy-back[4] purposes (Wright, 1981:33; Shields, 1981:72). It should come as no surprise to anyone that almost everyone believes in "cracking down" on illegal sales.

*Public attitudes toward a handgun ban.* It is clear that "a sizeable majority of the U.S. population disapproves of the notion of an outright ban[5] on the ownership of handguns" (Wright, 1981:34). In the Caddell survey, 62 percent of the respondents opposed the idea while only 38 percent favored a ban of this type. And 83 percent of the respondents in the national survey conducted by Decision Making Information (DMI) Inc. disagreed with the statement that "no private individual should be allowed to own a handgun" (Wright, 1981:33-34). In particular, survey data do not argue well for the matter of compliance. Ninety-two percent of the DMI respondents thought that half or less of the gun owners would obey a federal ban on handguns (Kleck et al., 1982:43). In a 1977 Illinois study, 73 percent of the gun owners said they would not comply with a law requiring them to turn in their handguns to the federal government (Kleck, 1984a:32; Bordua, 1984:57-58). When a handgun ban was left up to the voters in a 1976 Massachusetts referendum on the issue, it was defeated by a 2-1 margin (Shields, 1981:72).

# NOTES

1   In many jurisdictions, even if the cases are dismissed due to illegal searches, the guns in question are confiscated by the police and destroyed.

2   Seemingly contradictory because if there is widespread noncompliance by ordinary citizens, then outlaws will not be the only ones to have guns; and if only outlaws have guns under a handgun ban, then wherein lies the predicted widespread "flouting" of the law by the general public?

3   Which might very well include compensating citizens for their confiscated property.

4   The 1976 Massachusetts referendum to ban civilian possession of all handguns was purportedly defeated because 70 percent of the voters thought it would be too expensive for the state to buy back all handguns from the current owners.

5   The one notable exception is that 70 percent favored banning the production and sale of "cheap, low-quality handguns," i.e., Saturday Night Specials.

# 8

# Firearms, Self-Defense and Deterrence

---

In large part, the gun control controversy hinges on whether firearms (especially handguns) afford their owners and society any real protection from crime and violence. Ideally, it would be desirable to know if civilian ownership of firearms curtailed more crime than it caused. The full deterrent impact of armed citizens may be unmeasurable, however, because we do not know the number of crimes contemplated by criminals which are not executed (or attempted) because of their fear of confronting an armed victim. Nor can the social utility of firearms be resolved by the oft-observed correlation between increasing crime rates and increasing levels of gun ownership, due to the difficulty in determining cause and effect: High levels of violent crime may cause frightened citizens to arm themselves in response to the threat of crime and victimization. But alternatively, escalating gun ownership may contribute to high crime rates via the weapons-effect and by making more guns accessible to criminals through theft (Green, 1987:68; Benson, 1984:331,340). Are guns an efficacious defense against criminal violence? Or do they merely offer the illusion of protection while, in actuality, making people less safe in their homes by their very presence? The main sources of information for shedding light on the crime control aspects of firearms are discussed below.

## REASONS FOR OWNING GUNS

Two national surveys which obtained information on why citizens owned guns and their use of firearms were conducted in 1978 by Decision Making Information (DMI) and Cambridge Reports (the Caddell survey).[1] The findings from these two surveys—sponsored by organizations with opposite views on gun control—are remarkably consistent. DMI found that protection (self-defense) was the *primary* reason given by 1 out of every 5 gun owners for owning firearms (Wright, 1984:306). An additional 38 percent identified protection as a secondary reason, so that the defensive aspect of firearms was a salient consideration for almost two-thirds of all

61

gun owners. The Caddell survey, which focused exclusively on handguns,[2] found that 71 percent of the handgun owners owned them "for protection or self-defense" and 29 percent reported carrying their handguns with them for protection outside the home (Wright, 1981:28). Other surveys also indicate that about 45 percent of handgun owners cite protection as the *primary* reason for ownership (Kleck, 1988:4). (Women—young women and black women in particular—are much more likely to own guns solely for protection than are other groups (Bordua, 1984:61; Kleck, 1984b:107). Thus, "it is clear that defense or protection is a very common reason for owning guns in general, and that it is the *dominant* reason . . . for owning handguns in the United States."

## DEFENSIVE USE OF GUNS

The DMI survey found that around 15 percent of the American electorate, or about 13 million Americans as of 1978, had "used" (not necessarily fired) a gun to protect themselves, other family members, or property at some time in their lives. Thirteen percent of the Caddell handgun owners said they ever "had to use" their weapons in self-defense, which usually meant that they fired their handguns (Wright, 1981:28). It therefore appears that 2-6 percent of the total adult population have actually fired a handgun in self-defense (Wright, 1981:28-31). Ten percent of the DMI respondents could recall a situation where they "needed a gun but no gun was available" (Wright, 1981:30).

*Defensive use may exceed criminal misuse of guns.* A 1981 Hart poll of 1228 registered voters revealed that 4 percent of the respondents had used a handgun within the last five years to protect their person or property. Extrapolating this 4 percent figure to the number of households in 1980, Kleck found that there were an estimated 645,000 defensive uses[3] of handguns against persons by a household member in 1980 (Kleck, 1988:2). In the same year there were about 580,000 instances when handguns were used by criminals *to* commit crime. "Thus, the best available evidence suggests that handguns may be used about as often for defensive purposes as for criminal purposes. . ." (Kleck, 1988:4). Guns of all types (including long guns) were estimated to be used defensively about one million times a year, which is roughly equivalent to the total number of arrests (988,000) made for violent crime and burglary in 1980 (Kleck, 1988:4). Some individuals have rejected Kleck's defensive-use figures and conclusions because they were not based on new research and because the term "self-protection" was defined so broadly in the original survey that respondents could respond positively "if they heard a noise in the basement and checked it out with a gun" (*New Republic,* 1988:9).

*Felons killed by citizens.* Utilizing a combination of other data sources, Kleck arrived at a national estimate that in 1980, between 1,500-3,000 felons were legally killed by armed civilians in self-defense or for related-legally justified reasons; an additional 8,700-16,600 criminals were legally wounded under the same circumstances. If these figures are accurate, then civilians kill (and injure) far more felons annually than do police officers, i.e., criminals have more to fear from armed victims than from the police (Kleck, 1988:5).

## FACTORS BEHIND DEFENSIVE GUN OWNERSHIP

*Fear of crime and victimization.* Studies indicate that the fear of crime, victimization, and crime levels are all related to protective gun (especially handgun) ownership (Kleck, 1984b:107-113). Defensive gun ownership, for example, is higher among persons living in high-crime than in low-crime areas (Wright, 1984:309). Much defensive ownership is motivated by the *anticipation* of becoming a victim of crime (expected victimization) rather than actual prior victimization (Wright, 1984:309): "the perceived threat of victimization increases the probability of owning a gun for protection" (Young, 1987:55). This was confirmed in Clotfelter's study of the effects of the riots which occurred in the 1960s. His analysis in five states indicated that civil disorders "have played a significant role in the growth of handgun purchases" (Clotfelter, 1981:436). In effect, defensive handgun acquisition was a response to citizen perceptions and fears that they might be the next targets of rampant criminality (Clotfelter, 1981:438).

*Police cannot always protect you.* The explosion in (reported) crime and demand for police services has literally overwhelmed the police capacity to respond to them. In 1981 there were 700,000 calls for help by citizens in Dade County (Florida) but only 200,000 received any police response. "A half million Dade County residents' pleas for police aid went unanswered" (*A Question of Self-Defense,* 1987). And since the great majority of police work is reactive rather than proactive, the police usually arrive at the crime scene too late to prevent or mitigate the victimization. A Detroit study found that the probability of owning guns for personal protection was inversely related to the public's confidence in the ability of the police (and courts) to adequately protect them from crime. For example, citizens with the most confidence in the police were about 38 percent *less* likely to own guns for protection than those who were least confident (Young, 1987:54-55). When confidence in the police is weak, citizens feel they are more vulnerable to victimization and are more apt to rely on individualistic, self-help responses, such as arming themselves. By their very nature, civil disorders reduce confidence in the official agencies of collective security and cause people to rely on their own devices for assuring their personal safety (Kleck, 1984b:111).

*Reassurance factor.* Guns provide a source of psychological "reassurance" even among citizens who are not especially concerned about the fear of crime of being victimized. Almost half of all DMI respondents said yes to the question, "Do you personally feel that the presence of a gun in your home would make you feel more secure, or not?" (Bordua, 1984:59-60). Guns are not purchased for the purpose of using them defensively as soon and as often as possible. Rather, firearms are viewed as a contingency measure "just in case" family members find themselves in a dangerous situation, no matter how unlikely the prospect (Kleck, 1984a:39; Clotfelter, 1981:429). The mere possession of firearms makes its beneficiaries feel safer within the confines of their homes and have less anxiety about the fear of crime (Bruce-Briggs, 1976:40). Much like an insurance policy, "The chief benefit of defensive gun ownership is not the actual *use* of guns for defense against criminals, but rather the peace of mind that is produced by the knowledge that the gun is available and *could* be used for defensive purposes if needed" (Kleck, 1984a:34).

## ORLANDO RAPE STUDY

Perhaps the best evidence of firearms deterrence comes from the Orlando rape experiment. After the city's rape rate tripled from 1965 to 1966, the Orlando Police Department offered a training course in handgun self-defense, which was taken by 6,000 women between October 1966 through April 1967. The media gave extraordinary publicity to the program, stressing that Orlando's female population was now "armed and dangerous" to would-be rapists.

A year after the program began Orlando's rape rate dropped by almost 90 percent. By comparisons, rape rates in the surrounding areas and for the state as a whole were virtually unchanged or on the upswing during the same period (*A Question of Self-Defense,* 1987; Benson, 1984:341). The experiment also had a carry-over impact on reducing Orlando's burglary rate by 24 percent because "burglaries would seem to be the next most likely crime target to be effected by a program that trained women in firearms use . . ." (Green, 1987:73-74; Kates, 1976a:28). These results are even more noteworthy because there were no data indicating whether the training course lead more women to acquire handguns or to actually use firearms against criminals in self-protection (Kleck, 1988:15).

*Criminal-awareness factor.* In order for civilian gun ownership to operate as a deterrent, criminals must know, believe or be aware that the victim may be or is likely to be armed. It is obviously not a matter of common knowledge to criminals that a particular homeowner, woman or any other victim has a gun handy; so that burglars, for example, are not likely to be deterred from victimizing a particular residence. But criminals may very easily *become* aware that certain neighborhoods, regions of the country, social groups or types of places are, in the aggregate, heavily armed or more likely to be armed (Kleck, 1984a:35). A common way that criminals learn about the likelihood that certain types of victims will be armed is through the mass media, as well as by experience. The highly publicized Orlando program, for example, amounted to a "gun awareness" program which put criminals on notice that a specific category of potential victims was likely to be armed, able and willing to use their weapons (Kleck, 1988:13; Benson, 1984:341). Anything that makes criminals believe or feel that the risk of encountering an armed victim is too high to take can be the awareness-link to deterrence: Kennesaw's mandatory gun ownership law, all highly publicized gun training programs, the relaxation of strict gun control policies, seeing citizens strolling in public places with handguns strapped to their waists, having criminal acquaintances who were shot by homeowners, and newspaper accounts "playing up" cases in which armed citizens wound or kill criminals (Green, 1987:77).

## CRIMINALS' VIEWS OF ARMED CITIZENS

Firearm deterrence can be gleaned from the Felon Survey men's attitudes toward and experiences with armed victims (see Box 8.1). When contemplating criminality activity, an identical proportion said they worried about getting shot by their victim as by the police; and one-third were "scared off, shot at, wounded or captured by an armed victim" (Wright & Rossi, 1986:15,148). Two-fifths of the sample could recall at least one time when they decided not to commit a crime because they "knew or believed that the victim was carrying a gun" (Wright & Rossi, 1986:147). Among those who had ever actually encountered an armed victim, two-thirds said that they had also been deterred or thwarted by such an experience on at least one occasion (Wright & Rossi, 1986:155; Green, 1987:72).

---

**Box 8.1 The Criminal Speaks Out**

|  | % That Agree |
|---|---|
| 1. A criminal is not going to mess around with a victim that he knows is armed with a gun. | 56 |
| 2. A smart criminal always tries to find out whether his potential victim is armed. | 81 |
| 3. A store owner who is known to keep a gun on the premises is not going to get robbed very often. | 58 |
| 4. Most criminals are more worried about meeting an armed victim than they are about running into the police. | 57 |
| 5. One reason burglars avoid houses when people are at home is that they fear being shot. | 74 |

Source: James D. Wright and Peter H. Rossi, *Armed and Considered Dangerous,* New York: Aldine De Gruyter, 1986, p. 146.

---

The relevance of the felons' responses to deterrence has been questioned because the very fact that they were convicted criminals doing time indicates that none of their "experiences with armed victims has caused them to curtail their criminal activity as a whole" (Green, 1987:72). The authors of the Felon Survey, however, assert that their findings provide:

> at least some evidence that armed citizens abort or
> prevent at least some crime . . . [In] all cases, the
> majority opinion was that felons are made nervous by
> the prospect of encounter with an armed victim . . . a
> consistent pattern is that most criminals were at least
> as worried about confronting an armed victim as they
> were about confronting the police. Generally speaking,
> felons from states with proportionately more gun own-
> ers worried proportionately more about 'armed victim'
> encounters than did felons in other states (Wright &
> Rossi, 1986:153-154).

In support of this position, Kleck and Bordua correctly note that the gun-owning citizenry is certainly more omnipresent than the police, and the potential severity of private justice is at least as severe as that associated with formal punishment, which makes it entirely feasible "that private gun ownership currently exerts as much or more deterrent effect on criminals as do the activities of the criminal justice system" (Benson, 1984:343).

# GUNS IN HOME NO DETERRENT TO CRIME?

Gun controllers maintain that while guns may provide citizens the illusion of safety, in actuality gun ownership does not prevent or deter criminal victimization, i.e., handguns are virtually useless in the homefront battle against crime (Kleck, 1984a:34; Anderson, 1986:234). As to the first point, Kleck has aptly noted that if enhanced "psychological" safety were the only benefit of defensive gun ownership:

> in modern society [that] is *not* a trivial benefit . . . If gun
> ownership provides some peace of mind for people who
> live in areas with high nighttime burglary rates, then
> these guns provide a valuable service even if they are not
> actually used (Kleck et al., 1982:6).

*Cleveland study of accidental firearm deaths.* The claim that "statistics clearly demonstrate the bankruptcy of the self-defense argument" refers to data which purportedly show that loaded guns kept in the house for self-defense are much more likely to endanger gun owners and family members than to protect them from criminals (Drinan, 1976:49). This position stems from a Cleveland study which compared accidental firearm fatalities with guns used to kill felons from 1958-1973, the great majority of which involved handguns:

> Our data suggest that guns in the home are more danger-
> ous than useful to the homeowner and his family who
> keep them to protect their persons and property. During
> the period surveyed in this study, only 23 burglars, rob-
> bers or intruders who were not relatives or acquaintances
> were killed by guns in the hands of persons who were
> protecting their homes. During this same interval, 6
> times as many fatal firearm accidents occurred in the
> home. We conclude that a loaded firearm in the home is
> more likely to cause an accidental death than to be used
> as a lethal weapon against an intruder (Rushforth,
> 1975:504).

A similar study from 1978-1983 in King County (Wash.) of 398 firearm related deaths[4] which occurred where the guns were kept made essentially the points:

> For every case of self-protection homicide involving a
> firearm kept in the home, there were 1.3 accidental
> deaths, 4.6 criminal homicides, and 37 suicides involving

firearms . . . Even after excluding suicide deaths, guns in
the home were involved in the death of a household
member 18 times more often than in the death of a
stranger (Kellerman & Reay, 1986:1557,1559).

*Shortcomings of Cleveland study.* The Cleveland study was beset with
numerous flaws. Incredibly, the study included firearm *suicides* within the
category of "accidental" deaths. According to Silver and Kates, who reana-
lyzed the data, if suicides are deleted from the count, then the probability of
residents killing felons with handguns are several times higher than handguns contributing to a family member's accidental death (Wright,
1984:317). In addition, almost half of the self-defensive use of guns in the
home was excluded on the grounds that the criminal intruder killed was not
a total stranger to the home defender (*Ten Myths About Gun Control*,
1987:4-5)!

The major flaw in all such studies is that "the [proper] measure of the
effectiveness of self defense is not in the number of bodies [of criminals]
piled up on doorsteps," since only 5-10 percent of defensive gun use results
in the intruder's or assailant's death (Kleck, 1984a:35; *Justice Reporter,*
1981:7). A more valid assessment of firearm deterrence would take into
consideration the number of crimes against household members and property that were prevented or thwarted by virtue of armed homeowners, e.g.,
offenders who were driven or scared off, wounded, captured by the victim
or held at bay until the police arrived (Bruce-Briggs, 1976:39). Moreover,
many cases of deterrence are not self-defense but rather instances of armed
citizens coming to the aid of their neighbors or who, as good Samaritans,
help strangers being attacked. The vast majority of defensive gun uses are
not reported to the police, either because the victim can not provide a
description of the offender or because the citizen was carrying or possessed
an illegal gun (Kates, 1976a:28).

## GUNS NO DETERRENT TO BURGLARY OR ROBBERY?

Critics of protective gun ownership point out that since almost all burglaries (90%) occur in unoccupied dwellings, firearms are of no avail in preventing this particular offense. Reflecting this viewpoint, the Eisenhower
Commission concluded that "the gun is rarely an effective means of protecting
the home against either the burglar or the robber: the former avoids confronta-
tion and the latter confronts too swiftly" (Kates, 1976a:27). Some critics
believe that the presence of a gun in the home, if known by the burglar,
"would probably constitute an inducement, rather than a deterrent, to the commission of a crime. A gun in an empty house is a lure" (Drinan, 1976:49).

A more plausible interpretation, however, is that burglars confine their activities to empty premises because they want to avoid confronting armed victims. Three-quarters of the Felon Survey men agreed with the statement "One reason burglars avoid houses when people are at home is that they fear being shot" (Wright & Rossi, 1986:146). Some of the professional robbers interviewed by Conklin began their careers as burglars but switched to other crimes because of "the risk of being trapped in a house by the police or an *armed occupant*" (Kleck, 1984a:37). A convict in Atlanta explained that before commiting a crime, he did an extensive casing of each victim's situation "to ensure myself that there wasn't a gun on the premises except my own" (Wright, 1984:311). A year after Kennesaw's mandatory gun ownership ordinance, the burglary rate dropped by 89 percent compared to a 10 percent decrease in the burglary rate for the state as a whole (Green, 1987:75; Kleck, 1988:15). And when the police force went on strike in Albuquerque (New Mexico) the crime rate *decreased* because frightened citizens armed themselves and stood vigil over their homes and businesses: while criminals knew that, if apprehended, free lawyers would "skate" them out of court, they "had no stomach at all for facing indignant citizens protecting their own property with the same force the criminals used to steal it" (Ayoob, 1981:14).

*Taking aim at robbers.* The Eisenhower Commission's remark that robbery "confronts too quickly" refers to situations in which potential victims do not have immediate access to firearms. As such, it does not apply to armed merchants as a category, who foil an appreciable number of robberies each year (Kates, 1976a:27). In Chicago in a typical year, more criminals are shot by storeowners and other armed citizens than by the entire police force (Ayoob, 1981:4). Firearm training programs for retail merchants have resulted in dramatic decreases in robbery wherever such efforts have been tried (Kleck, 1988:13). For example, after police ran a high-profile firearms training course for merchants in Highland Park (Michigan), there were no robberies in the next 4 months compared with 190 holdups in the preceding 4 months (Ayoob, 1981:15; Green, 1987:76). And in Detroit, after a grocer's organization started offering firearm training through "gun clinics" and grocers shot seven robbers, grocery store robbery dropped by almost 90 percent (Green, 1987:76).

## ARE ARMED RESISTERS "ASKING FOR TROUBLE"?

Opponents of protective gun use believe that armed resistance to offenders exacerbates the outcome of victimization, especially be making victims more vulnerable to injury. While this complex issue will not be resolved here, the evidence presented below suggests otherwise (See Table 8.1).

**Table 8.1 Attack, Injury and Crime Completion Rates in Robbery and Assault Incidents, by Self-Protection Method, U.S., 1979-85***

| Method of Self-Protection | Completed | *Robbery* Attacked | Injured | *Assault*[†] Completed | Attacked |
|---|---|---|---|---|---|
| Used gun | 30.9% | 25.2% | 17.4% | 23.2% | 12.1% |
| Used knife | 35.2 | 55.6 | 40.3 | 46.4 | 29.5 |
| Used other weapon | 28.9 | 41.5 | 22.0 | 41.4 | 25.1 |
| Used physical force | 50.1 | 75.6 | 50.8 | 82.8 | 52.1 |
| Tried to get help/ frighten offender | 63.9 | 73.5 | 48.9 | 55.2 | 40.1 |
| Threatened/reasoned with offender | 53.7 | 48.1 | 30.7 | 40.0 | 24.7 |
| Nonviolent resist, incl. evasion | 50.8 | 54.7 | 34.9 | 40.0 | 25.5 |
| Other measures | 48.5 | 47.3 | 26.5 | 36.1 | 20.7 |
| Any self-protection | 52.1 | 60.8 | 38.2 | 49.5 | 30.7 |
| No self-protection | 88.5 | 41.5 | 24.7 | 39.9 | 27.3 |
| Total | 65.4 | 53.7 | 33.2 | 47.3 | 29.9 |

*Analysis of incident files of 1979-1985 National Crime Survey public use tapes (ICPSR, 1987b). Table adapted from: Gary Kleck, "Crime Control Through the Private Use of Armed Force," *Social Problems,* February 1988, p. 4 (Reprinted with permission of author).
[†]For assault, "completion" is the same as "injury."

Data from National Crime Panel surveys between 1979-1985 show that (1) a smaller proportion of robberies and assaults were completed when victims of each crime used guns or other weapons for self-protection, than if victims didn't resist at all or used non-lethal methods of resistance; and (2) robbery victims and assault victims who resisted with guns "were less likely either to be attacked or injured than victims who responded any other way, including those who did not resist at all" (Kleck, 1988:7-9). For example, only 12 percent of the gun resisters in assault and 17 percent in robbery suffered any kind of injury. By comparison, twice as many assault victims and 50 percent more robbery victims who reacted passively were injured. In addition, a Justice Department 26-city survey involving 32,000 rapes found that the rapes were "unsuccessful" (not completed) in 97 percent of the cases where women used or brandished guns or knives to protect themselves.[5] By comparison, other types of self-protective measures were less likely to thwart completion of the offense, such as physical resistance, attracting attention or trying to reason with the rapist (McDermott, 1979:31).

What about cases where victims respond with forceful self-protection (armed or physical resistance) and *are* injured? Under these circumstances, is armed resistance somehow responsible for the injuries inflicted, i.e., does it provoke criminals to escalate the level of violence? Data from a 1984 National Crime Panel survey found that in robbery cases where the victims were actually assaulted, forceful self-protective actions never preceded the attack; and "where forceful self-protective acts were accompanied by attacks [injuries] on the victim, few incidents support the contention that the victim's defensive action provoked the attack" (Kleck, 1988:9). Of course, guns must be directly accessible in order to be an effective means of self-protection. Robberies which occur on the street against unarmed victims who forcefully resist may indeed increase the victim's chances for serious injury or death (Wright, 1984:313). But there is nothing in the data presented here to indicate that victims who use guns to ward off violent crime are any worse for doing so.

## NOTES

[1]   The DMI survey was commissioned by the National Rifle Association, and the Caddell survey was done for the Center for the Study and Prevention of Handgun Violence.

[2]   The DMI question on reason-for-ownership referred to all firearms, including long guns.

[3]   Besides firing at someone, defensive-uses included pointing, displaying, brandishing, referring to guns, and firing warning shots.

[4]   71 percent by handguns.

[5]   The Justice Department cautioned against drawing any firm conclusions about the advisability of armed resistance to rape because of the small number of cases on which the 97 percent figure was based.

# 9

# Mandatory Sentences

## MANDATORY SENTENCES FOR WHOM?

When it comes to gun crime, conservatives and liberals alike endorse the idea of mandatory prison sentences but part ways over to whom they should be applied. Conservatives call for the imposition of mandatory sentences for those who *use* firearms to commit crime, i.e., the criminal-element whose gun use is deliberate, calculated and part of a history of violent crime. This reflects the conservative view that firearms misuse is a "crime problem" rather than a "gun problem," that such laws will inhibit the sanctioned offenders from recidivating, and that by example it will deter other would-be criminals from gun crime. A number of states do have mandatory sentences for gun crimes, or they have "enhancement" statutes which mandate additional periods of incarceration for gun crimes over and above the penalty prescribed for the basic offense (Gettinger, 1980:14; Anderson, 1986:235).

While not denying the value of requiring stiff sentences for gun offenders, liberals believe the thrust should be on *preventing* gun crime rather than responding to it after-the-fact. Accordingly, mandatory sentences would be imposed for the illegal possession/carrying of firearms, i.e., on the non-criminal element who keep a firearm on their person or in the car with no specific criminal purpose in mind (Gettinger, 1980:14). These "casual carriers" are said to be "looking for trouble" because many of the guns will end up being used on the spur-of-the-moment to settle arguments or for opportunistic crime. By making certainty and severity of punishment for illegal carrying a salient reality, the expectation is that mandatory sentences will lead to a reduction in the incidence of gun-related crimes (Pierce & Bowers, 1981:131).

## MASSACHUSETTS BARTLEY-FOX LAW

The Massachusetts Bartley-Fox law, which took effect in April 1975, imposed a one-year mandatory jail sentence for anyone convicted of carrying an unlicensed firearm outside their home or place of business (Rossman et al., 1980:151). The law was intended to nip gun-related crime in the bud by intervening at the critical point at which the decision to carry was made (Pierce & Bowers, 1981:131). Bartley-Fox (BF) specifically prohibited suspended sentences and probation or parole, which was widely publicized in a $2 million advertising campaign based on the slogan "No one can get you out." Previously, illegal-carrying was punishable by a fine, suspended sentence, or (rarely imposed) brief incarceration (Pierce & Bowers, 1981:122).

*Effectiveness of Bartley-Fox.* Northeastern University researchers who conducted a major evaluation of the law concluded that "gun-related violent crime rates fell dramatically in Massachusetts between 1974 and 1976, suggesting that Bartley-Fox had an extraordinarily large deterrent effect," at least in the short run (Pierce & Bowers, 1981:123). In particular, the law was found to have had an impact on assaults, robberies and homicides committed with guns (see Box 9.1 for highlights of results in Boston, the main focus of the evaluation). However, although BF apparently induced some individuals to leave their guns at home—thereby preventing their committing gun assaults when spontaneously provoked—it did not keep them out of assaultive situations and resorting to less lethal weapons at hand (Pierce & Bowers, 1981:120). "My suspicion is that people went about their lives without a gun and encountered the same type of trouble. This time they had to fight with the weapons in the environment—beer mugs, bar stools— instead of guns" (Gettinger, 1980:15). The reason that non-gun assaults increased was probably because "without a gun around, people feel freer to strike out" (Gettinger, 1980:15).

*Impact underestimated.* The law's full impact may have been obscured because the publicity surrounding BF encouraged more citizens to report minor ("without-battery"[1]) gun offenses that were previously considered a private matter. This was confirmed by the finding that gun assaults resulting in injury ("with battery")—which are less subject to reporting changes and thus a better measure of deterrence—declined by 37 percent in Boston between 1974-1976, more so than in any of the control areas (Pierce & Bowers, 1981:129,131). BF was judged a success in other areas as well. There was evidence of greater citizen compliance in obtaining the necessary permits before carrying firearms in public. And there was no evidence that the police avoided enforcing the law or did so in an unfair or discriminatory manner (Rossman, 1980:153). Sherman points out that BF may have contributed to police safety, as the proportion of gun assaults on Boston police declined from 7 percent in 1974 to 2 percent in 1976 (Sherman, 1980:164-165).

---

**Box 9.1 Effects of Bartley-Fox Law in Boston[†]**

- Gun homicides declined by 56 percent, moreso than in any of the control sites, and there was no displacement, i.e., non-gun homicides dropped (by 20%) as well.
- Gun assaults dropped by 14 percent the first year, a larger decrease than in any of the 13 control areas. However, there was a 40 percent increase in non-gun armed[††] assaults, which was more than twice the increase registered in any of the control areas (see text discussion of this point)..
- Gun robberies decreased by 36 percent, which compared very favorably with results in the control jurisdictions; but there was considerable displacement to non-gun armed robberies.

[†]Unless otherwise noted, the results are based on the two-year follow-up study (1974-1976) conducted by Northeastern University researchers.
[††]E.g., knives, blunt instruments.

---

*Drop in convictions.* Prosecution problems arising under BF made abundantly clear that "mandatory sentences are by no means inevitable sentences" (Sherman, 1980:167). Facing certain and tough penalties, almost all defendants demanded jury trials[2] instead of pleading guilty to the original carrying charge as before (Gettinger, 1980:15). In 1974 (before BF), 71 percent of the gun-carrying cases disposed of in Superior Court were convictions, which fell to 44 percent in 1976. This was because (a) legally weak cases were prosecuted, and lost, under the pressure of the law to make an example out of each violator, and (b) even if the defendant's guilt was clear-cut, juries and judges were reluctant to convict if they felt that sending "decent citizens" with no record to jail for a year was unduly harsh or inappropriate (Ayoob, 1981:18; Bruce-Briggs, 1976:45).

In the first case brought under BF, a "little old lady" distributing religious material in a tough section of Boston was arrested for carrying a pistol in her lunch bag, and the court dismissed all charges on patently dubious legal grounds (Gettinger, 1980:15). In another case observed by the Northeastern researchers, the defendant made no effort to contest the facts of the case but instead did everything possible to convince the jury that he was not "the sort of person" who deserved spending a year in jail; he didn't (Rossman, 1980:162). Moreover, gun carriers could circumvent BF completely through plea bargaining, which was unaffected by the law, e.g., defendants could plead guilty to the reduced charge of "illegal possession" which did not carry a mandatory sentence (Rossman, 1980:163).

Whether BF had any significant or lasting impact on crime in Boston or throughout the state remains a highly debatable issue, with some authorities convinced that the "two major studies of the BF law have data limitations which render most conclusions tentative at best" (Ayoob, 1981:18). The Northeastern researchers acknowledge that the law may have achieved its effect "primarily through its 'announced' intent [advertising campaign] rather than its actual implementation" and, consequently, they "draw no conclusions about the effect of the 'mandatory' nature of the law (Pierce & Bowers, 1981:137). Commenting on the fact that there was a shift back to street gun robbery by 1977, Blackman suggests it was because, by then, the criminals realized that "Bartley-Fox was a greater threat to their potential victims—disarming them for safer street robberies—than to the violent criminals themselves" (Rossman, 1980:153; Blackman, 1981:13).

## NOTES

1    Situations in which guns were displayed or used to threaten, but not fired or used as a club.

2    Only one-fifth took their chances with a jury before the law was passed.

# 10

# Gun Control through Strict Liability

## DOCTRINE OF STRICT LIABILITY

The theory behind "product liability" law is that if a manufacturer produces a product that is defective or unreasonably dangerous, they can be sued on the grounds of *strict liability:* the manufacturer is legally responsible (liable) for the harmful consequences of its products even though there was no intent to injure anyone ("Handguns and Product Liability," 1984:1921).

The courts rely on two tests for deciding the issue of strict liability, either of which is a prerequisite for recovering damages from the manufacturer: (1) Under the *consumer-expectations* test, "a product may be found defective in design if the plaintiff establishes that the product failed to perform as safely as an ordinary consumer would expect when used in an intended or reasonably foreseeable manner" (*Barker v. Lull Engineering Co.* 20 Cal. 3d 413, 573 P.2d 443, 143 Cal. Rptr. 225 [1978]). (2) Under the *risk-utility* test, a product is considered "unreasonably dangerous" if its design or performance is so faulty, unsafe or hazardous that the chance of incurring serious injury or illness from using the product ["risk"] outweighs whatever value or collective benefits to consumers ["utility"] the product may have (Davies, 1986:480-481; Hardy, 1987:68; "Handguns and Product Liability," 1984:13). Under either test, plaintiffs have successfully applied strict liability to manufacturers for accidental injuries and deaths associated with a variety of products: faulty automobile steering mechanisms, non-fire-retardant children's clothing, contraceptive devices, mobile homes designed without adequate fire-escape exits, and guns which accidentally discharged because the safety lock did not work or because of some other failure attributable to design defect (Hardy, 1987:66-67,70; Halbrook, 1983:358). In all of these examples, the companies were strictly liable because their product met the consumer-expectations test and/or the risk-utility test—their products did not work, operate or do what they were "supposed to."

## EXPANDING STRICT LIABILITY
## TO FIREARMS PROCEDURES

In recent years, gun control advocates have attempted to stretch the theory of strict liability to cover handgun manufacturers whose products are used by *criminals* who intentionally injure or kill their victims (Hardy, 1987:66-67). The argument for extending strict liability to manufacturers for handgun crime injury is that handguns *per se*—as an entire product line—are unreasonably dangerous by any measure of strict liability (except the consumer-expectations test[1]): by the risk-utility test, by their "defective design" (concealability) which makes them a threat to public safety, and because the manufacturer's inability to keep handguns out of the wrong hands constitutes a "marketing defect" (Turley, 1982:49; "Handguns and Product Liability," 1984:1912).

*Risk-utility analysis.* The main justification advanced for "expansive" strict liability is the contention that handguns pass the risk-utility test, i.e., the damage handguns do outweighs their social value. However, it could just as easily be argued that a risk-utility analysis leads to the opposite conclusion. The refusal of state and federal government to ban handguns, and the regulation of firearms production and sales through licensing requirements implies a legislative consensus that handguns have a social utility which overrides its attendant risks ("Handguns and Product Liability," 1984:1925). The huge number of handguns in circulation which are not misused, citizen reliance on handguns for self-defense, the reassurance value of handguns, Second Amendment considerations—these factors cannot be dismissed or minimized in any risk-utility analysis. Moreover, handgun fatalities are a miniscule risk when compared to deaths caused by other common commodities (Hardy, 1987:72,78). Because drunk drivers kill twice as many people a year as handgun homicides do, that does not make alcohol or automobiles unreasonably dangerous products which society should rid itself of through strict liability ("Handguns and Product Liability," 1984:1917). Such benefits as accrue to handguns do so precisely because, by their very nature, they *are* dangerous items (Hardy, 1987:76; "Handguns and Product Liability," 1984:1916). Whether a product is unreasonably dangerous or performing its proper function cannot be based on the use to which it is put in any particular case or situation, since virtually any product—no matter how well designed or innocuous—can be grossly misused ("Handguns and Product Liability," 1984:1017).

*Defect in distribution.* Another rationale for expansive strict liability is that the unsafe manner in which firearm companies market their wares—making it all too easy for "an obviously irresponsible person" to buy a handgun—constitutes a "defect" in distribution (improper-distribution) (Lapp, 1987:179; "Handguns and Product Liability," 1984:1923). But even *if* the defective-distribution claim were credible, the gun *dealers* are the more appropriate targets of strict liability, because they are in the best position to prevent the "defect" of handguns falling into the wrong hands (Hardy, 1987:68). The federal government recognized the role of gun dealers in preventing "improper distribution" of firearms, through legislation discussed earlier in this monograph. The courts have, on occasion, imposed strict liability on dealers for selling guns to individuals they "should have known" would use them to commit crimes or customers who were prohibited from owning firearms ("Handguns and Product Liability," 1984:1924). Other than this, the courts have held that a purchaser's subsequent misuse of a firearm is an unforeseeable event so far as the gun dealer is concerned. Because the criminal use of handguns is even more unforeseeable from the manufacturer's vantage point, they cannot be considered the "proximate cause" of the victim's injuries and, hence, are insulated against strict liability (Halbrook, 1983:356): the current law "erects no duty upon a manufacturer of a non-defective [handgun] to anticipate the various unlawful acts possible through the misuse of that item" (Hardy, 1987:81; Wagner, 1988:17).

*Saturday Night Specials.* During a robbery in a grocery store where he worked, Olen Kelly was shot in the chest with a Rohm-made .38 revolver. Kelly subsequently filed suit against Rohm Gesellschaft, the manufacturer, alleging that the company should be held strictly liable for his injury because this type of weapon was an unreasonably dangerous product (Brown, 1986:1333). In *Kelly v. R.G. Industries,* the Maryland Court of Appeals became the first jurisdiction to recognize a new area of strict liability directly applicable to firearm manufacturers for the criminal misuse of their products (*Kelly v. R.G. Industries,* 497 A.2d 1143 [Md. 1985]). Utilizing the flexibility of the common law to find "solutions to pressing societal problems," the court, in effect,[2] found ample evidence for singling out Saturday Night Specials as unreasonably dangerous products subject to manufacturer's strict liability. SNSs are tailor-made for criminal use because of their distinctive characteristics; both Maryland state law and federal policy behind the Gun Control Act of 1968 supports the view that SNSs "have little or no legitimate purpose in today's society," and they have minimal utility for self-protection because of their unreliability and inaccuracy (Lapp, 1987:187; Steffey, 1986:157). Significantly, the *Kelly* court had no difficulty in declaring that SNS manufacturers know or ought to know that their product's main use is for criminal consumption, i.e., the criminogenic character of this particular item is entirely foreseeable and predictable on the part of firearms manufacturers (Davies, 1986:484). Accordingly, the Court held that on the basis of their widespread criminal use and "virtual absence of legitimate uses . . . it is entirely consistent with public policy to hold the manufacturers and sellers of Saturday Night Specials strictly liable[3] to innocent person who suffer gunshot injuries from the criminal use of their products" (Lapp, 1987:188). The *Kelly* decision represents a precedent-setting endorsement of the position that "the manufacturer and seller of a SNS should be held strictly liable because the societal risks presented by such handguns far outweigh their benefits, if any benefits exist at all" (Lapp, 1987:181).

## PROPRIETY OF "JUDICIAL" GUN CONTROL

Litigation may be an efficient and effective vehicle for dealing with gun control because judges and juries are more immune from the political pressures of the gun lobby. There are those, however, who view strict liability as improper "judicial" gun control which subverts the will of the people, that is, as a transparent attempt by liberals to fall back on the courts because they have not been able to achieve their goals through the legislative process ("Handguns and Product Liability," 1984:1925). Political ideology aside, it is legitimate to raise the question of whether such far-reaching, major extensions of strict liability to handgun abuse should be implemented by judicial fiat rather than the democratic process, and whether the judiciary is equipped to do the job ("Handguns and Product Liability," 1984:1925; Lapp, 1987:181). "No jury or judge could possibly ascertain what effect outlawing handguns would have; . . . yet one must answer precisely this question to determine whether the risks of handguns outweigh their utility" ("Handguns and Product Liability," 1984:1927).

## NOTES

1    Handguns fail the consumer-expectations test because "the risks involved in marketing handguns are not greater than reasonable consumers expect."

2    Technically, the *Kelly* decision was not predicated on the risk-utility test, but the underlying rationale of the holding amounts to a de facto acceptance that Saturday Night Specials are unreasonably dangerous.

3    To win the case, the plaintiff must still convince the jury that the handgun involved was a "SNS."

# 11

# Taking Aim at Assault Rifles:
# The Next Wave of Gun Control

## THE STOCKTON MASSACRE

On January 17, 1989, Patrick Purdy, a 24-year-old alcoholic drifter, drove up to the Cleveland Elementary School in Stockton (Ca.), walked over to the crowded playgrounds where 450 children were at midday recess, hoisted his Chinese-made AK-47 rifle, and opened fire on the group, getting off 100 rounds in barely two minutes. The shooting spree left five children dead and 29 wounded. Then Purdy killed himself with a pistol shot to the head (*Newsweek*, 1989a). Using a false name and lying about his previous criminal record on federal Form 4493, Purdy purchased the $350 assault rifle in a sporting goods store in Oregon, which has neither a waiting period nor a background check (*New York Times*, 1989a).

*Focus on "assault rifles."* The AK-47 used by Purdy is just one of several types of semiautomatic "assault-style" weapons which, at that time, could be legally purchased over the counter just as easily as any other rifle or shotgun. These rapid-fire, military weapons fire one bullet each time the trigger is squeezed and can fire up to 70 rounds of bullets without reloading, which is done automatically. (Fully automatic weapons, commonly referred to as machine guns, fire a continuous stream of up to 600 bullets so long as the gun's trigger is depressed. Since 1934, their sale and possession has been federally banned to everyone except the police, military personnel and licensed collectors) (*Time*, 1989a; *New York Times*, 1989b). Once rare outside of the military, the Chinese made AK-47,[1] became legal here when the United States normalized relations with China (*Time*, 1989a). As frightening testimony of the popularity of the item, imports of AK-47s jumped from 4,000 in 1986 to 44,000 in 1988 (*Newsweek*, 1989b). A relatively inexpensive weapon ($250-$400), AK-47s are fast becoming the weapon of choice among street gang members and drug lords who use them against the police or rival drug peddlers. It is no coincidence that the phenomenal increase in semi-automatics parallels the takeover of entire sections of large cities by crack dealers (*Time*, 1989a).

*Assault-weapons ban gains momentum.* Public outrage over the Stockton massacre led to immediate action on two major fronts. First, bills to ban or tighten the manufacture, sale and/or possession of a variety of semiautomatic rifles were debated or pending in about 20 cities and 27 states throughout the country (*Law Enforcement News*, 1989; *U.S. News & World Report*, 1989a). On February 7, 1989, the Los Angeles City Council voted unanimously to immediately ban the sale and possession of semiautomatic weapons, an ordinance which Mayor Tom Brady signed into law[2] the next month (*National Law Journal*, 1989b). And in May 1989, California became the first state to outlaw assault rifles, making it illegal to manufacture, import or sell some 50 military-style weapons (*Newsweek*, 1989b; *New York Times*, 1989b). At the federal level, Sen. Howard Metzenbaum introduced a bill in Congress that would treat semiautomatics like machine guns, ban their further manufacture and importation, and subject those already in circulation to registration and tight restrictions on private transfers (*New York Times*, 1989b).

*Bush embargo.* Just a month before the schoolyard killings, President Bush, a life-time member of the NRA, told reporters that he was "not about to" impose a ban on semiautomatic weapons (*Time*, 1989c). At the urging of the new drug czar William Bennett, however, Bush reversed his stance and immediately imposed a temporary ban on five types of assault rifles imported by foreign manufacturers (*Newsweek*, 1989b). The next day Colt industries announced that, to be "consistent with U.S. Government policy" it would no longer sell its AK-15 assault rifle to the public at large (*Newsweek*, 1989b; *New York Times*, 1989c). Three weeks later, the original import ban was extended to 24 other semiautomatic models, thereby cancelling an order of 420,000 foreign assault rifles that had been scheduled for delivery in 1989 (*New York Times*, 1989d). As news of the embargo spread, gun shops across the country were inundated by gun fanciers and frightened citizens intent on buying assault rifles (at inflated prices) while the weapons were still legally available and in stock (*Time*, 1989a,c). In itself, the foreign embargo could hardly put a dent in the domestic semiautomatic market, because two-thirds of the estimated 500,000 to 1 million assault weapons in private hands are made by American companies, which were unaffected by the ban (*Time*, 1989c). Moreover, when imports of the Striker, a South-African made semiautomatic shotgun capable of firing 12 rounds in three seconds—"a truly murderous weapon that has no appropriate sport use"—was banned by the BATF in 1986, the gun was manufactured domestically and legally sold here under the trade name "Street Sweeper" (*Newsweek*, 1989b).

*Sporting-test.* The legal authority for the Administration's embargo was a provision of the Gun Control Act of 1968 that permits importing foreign-made weapons for civilian sale only when they are "generally recognized as particularly suitable for, or readily adaptable to *sporting purposes*." (emphasis added) The temporary halt on imports was indefinite, pending the outcome of a three-month review by the BATF to see if objective procedures could be developed for determining whether such weapons have any legitimate sporting use (*New York Times,* 1989d; *Time,* 1989c). Authorities recognized that the biggest hurdle would be in defining the difference between "assault" rifles and hunting rifles. Although assault weapons look more menacing, technically they are not very different from popular hunting rifles like the Remington 7400 (*New York Times,* 1989b).

## AK-47 CARNAGE IN LOUISVILLE

On September 14, 1989, Joseph Wesbecker, a disgruntled former employee, stalked into his old printing plant building carrying a gym bag containing hundreds of rounds of ammunition and several semiautomatic weapons, including the same type of AK-47 used by Purdy just eight months earlier. Looking for his bosses, Wesbecker took an elevator to the third floor where their offices were, "the doors opened and he started firing" wildly with the AK-47. The ensuing 30-minute shooting spree, randomly directed at anyone close by as he combed the building, left seven co-workers dead and 13 wounded, before Wesbecker killed himself with a 9mm semiautomatic Sig-Sauer pistol (*Newsweek,* 1989c).

Wesbecker had obtained his arsenal of weapons in an entirely legal manner—despite the fact that he was under treatment for mental illness, that he had attempted suicide on three previous occasions, that he was on permanent mental disability leave from his company, that his obsession with weapons was well-know, and that for a year he had openly talked about getting even with his superiors for perceived mistreatment ("I told them I'd be back") (*USA Today,* 1989). In May 1989, Wesbecker entered a Louisville gun shop and traded an AK-47 purchased earlier for a newer, more lethal model. On the federal registration form used in the transaction, Wesbecker truthfully answered "no" to the question whether he had ever been "committed to a mental institution." In the predictable cycle of events that followed, state legislators were "re-energized" into action, and gun control groups pressured Bush to ban the domestic manufacture and sale of all AK-47 type assault rifles; but the President declined to do so: "I have seen no evidence that a law banning a specific weapon is going to guard against this [kind of tragedy]" (*USA Today,* 1989).

## NRA UNDER SIEGE

In the aftermath of the Stockton and Louisville tragedies, the NRA came under intensified attack from all directions, with clear signs of eroding support among the police and the public. Public opinion polls taken at the time found that 72 percent of the public favored a permanent ban on assault weapons, and 54 percent of Americans thought the NRA "has too much influence in keeping stricter gun control laws from being passed" (*Time*, 1989b). Derisive criticism was leveled at the NRA's "same threadbare rhetoric about the rights of hunters; no serious hunter goes after deer with an Uzi or an AK-47" and the association's "criminals-will-always-get-assault rifles" overworked refrain (*Time*, 1989d). The only meaningful question seemed to be "Who really needs an AK-47, and why?", which was pointedly answered by L.A. Police Chief Daryl Gates, ordinarily regarded as a long-time *foe* of gun control: "There is no need for citizens to have highly sophisticated military assault rifles designed for the sole purpose of killing people on the battlefield" (*Time*, 1989a; *Newsweek*, 1989b). The combination of developments spurred by the Purdy onslaught posed the most serious, credible challenge to the NRA since its formation. The NRA's worst nightmare was apparently becoming true: gun control "nuts" were boldly going where no respectable reformers had gone before. The regulators had crossed the invisible line separating handguns—which were always fair game—from long guns, which were always considered exempt from gun control efforts (*Newsweek*, 1989b).

The NRA was uncharacteristically reticent in responding to the fallout from Stockton, choosing instead to adopt a low-profile strategy until the "public hysteria" surrounding the killings had run its course. Wayne LaPierre, the head of the NRA's lobbying division, simply and dutifully noted the difficulty of drawing the line between assault rifles and hunting rifles (*Newsweek*, 1989b). All of which is not to deny that the NRA was just waiting for a more opportune time to exploit their I-told-you-so "today SNSs, tomorrow long guns" dire prophecy. Gun control optimists, encouraged by the turn of events putting the NRA on the defensive for a change, clung to the belief that "the intensity of the urban movement against guns can only increase; in the long run, pro-gun forces will have to give way" (*U.S. News & World Report*, 1989b). By that time, though, every man, woman and child in America may have their own handgun, SNS, or assault rifle along with matching designer bullet-proof vests.

## NOTES

1    Which is a copy of the original, fully automatic Soviet AK-47.

2    Two other California cities, Stockton and Compton, and Cleveland (Ohio) rushed through similar legislation.

# 12

# Summary and Reflections
# on Gun Control

Data from the National Crime Survey reveal that, each year, firearms are used in the commission of some 837,000 crimes of violence.

The "weapons effect" theory stresses that merely having access to firearms can induce some individuals to engage in assaultive acts. The weapons effect purports to offer a scientific basis for the sentiment that "People Don't Kill People . . . Guns Do."

Handguns have been the traditional focus of gun control efforts because they are involved in a disproportionate amount of all violent crime and because of their widespread proliferation (an estimated 50-65 million) among the general public.

Saturday Night Specials, cheap and poorly constructed guns noted for their concealability, have been singled out by gun control advocates because confiscation studies indicate that they are used primarily to commit street crimes and have no socially legitimate purpose, i.e., they are "crime guns,"—a position adopted by the Maryland Court of Appeals in *Kelly v. R.G. Industries* (497 A.2d 1143 [Md. 1985]).

A policy of "permissive" licensing exists in most states, under which citizens (at least nominally) are legally entitled to own firearms provided they do not fall into any of the high-risk groups making them ineligible for gun possession.

Pursuant to their goal of taking handguns out of general circulation, the hallmarks of the gun controllers include "restrictive" licensing of handguns, banning SNSs, and tightening up the application and screening process for purchasing firearms.

The centerpiece of the federal Gun Control Act of 1968 was its provision prohibiting gun dealers from selling firearms to out-of-state residents in order to curtail the flow of weapons from one jurisdiction to another. Such "leakage" undermined the effectiveness of more stringent (restrictive) gun codes in adjacent or nearby states.

A major problem in keeping guns out of the wrong hands has been the absence of an effective verification system for determining, at the point of sale, whether would-be purchasers are in fact eligible to own firearms. A proposed national mandatory seven-day waiting period, during which an intensive applicant background check would be conducted, was thwarted by the NRA in 1988.

The first major change in federal gun policy in 20 years, the Firearms Owners Protection Act of 1986 (initiated by the NRA) made it easier for citizens to buy, sell, and transport firearms across state lines.

In 1981, Morton Grove (Illinois) became the first locality in the nation to ban the sale and possession of *all* handguns, which spurred towns and cities across the country to press for similar action.

In 1988, Maryland passed a law banning the manufacture and sale of Saturday Night Specials, becoming the first state to outlaw a particular category of handguns deemed to have no legitimate function or sporting-purpose value.

In what amounted to a resounding endorsement of the gun lobby ideology, in 1987 Florida became the largest urbanized state to pass a law allowing almost any law-abiding citizen to carry a concealed handgun in public.

Research findings on the effectiveness of gun control measures are inconsistent and inconclusive at best, yielding little consensus on the impact of such laws in general or of handgun restrictions in particular.

Comparisons of the homicide rates in foreign countries having very restrictive firearms laws with those in the United States shed very little light on whether gun control laws reduce crime in this country, because of vast cultural differences which may account for their lower homicide figures.

The Wright-Rossi felon survey (1986) of inmates in 10 states highlighted the difficulty of keeping firearms out of the hands of hardened criminals by regulating gun shop protocol. This is because only 1 out of 6 of the handgun-owning inmates had acquired their most-recent handgun via retail transactions from licensed dealers, and because of the relative absence of SNSs among the handguns preferred or carried by this group.

Private transfers of firearms from unlicensed citizens to persons known or suspected of being a convicted felon or in another high-risk group loom large in the criminal acquisition of firearms.

Under conditions of handgun scarcity or unavailability, would the criminal element or violence-prone individuals switch to less lethal weapons (like knives) to accomplish their objectives or to more lethal long guns instead? Data from the Wright-Rossi survey, as well as an analysis of homicide by "ordinary citizens," suggest that considerable long-gun substitution would occur, with its attendant more lethal consequences.

Any attempt at rigorous enforcement of a handgun ban among the general population would probably encounter monumental compliance obstacles. Short of total confiscation, there may be no foreseeable conditions under which enough present gun owners could be persuaded to give up their handguns for such a total ban to be workable.

While the public is deeply divided on the kind of gun control measures it wants and would accept, a sizeable majority of the population are clearly opposed to any outright ban on their right to possess handguns.

The weight of judicial rulings has established that there is no clear-cut, categorical *individual* "right to bear arms" derivable from the Second Amendment.

Data from a variety of sources suggest that armed citizens may indeed be a credible and formidable deterrent to crime commission and crime completion, thereby bolstering survey findings that protection and self-defense are the primary reasons for firearms ownership.

The "psychological reassurance" (insurance policy) factor among people who never have occasion to resort to their guns cannot be discarded or minimized as a real benefit of gun ownership.

The Massachusetts Bartley-Fox law, imposing a one-year mandatory jail term for anyone carrying an unlicensed firearm outside one's home or place of business, apparently had an impact on gun-related violent crime at least in the short-run.

Attempts to advance the cause of gun control by extending "strict liability" to firearms producers, distributors, and dealers raise troubling questions about the propriety of gun control by judicial fiat as well as the boundaries of third-party responsibility.

The focus on handguns and SNSs as the principal targets of gun control may come to be overshadowed by a rising demand to outlaw "assault" rifles, an issue on which it might be possible to achieve a much greater political consensus for action.

The core of the "gun control" controversy revolves around the tandem issues of how best to respond to the problem of gun crimes and of the right of citizens to have weapons for self-defense and home protection. Accidental deaths and suicides by firearms are somewhat peripheral concerns. For too long, the politics and the outcome of gun control efforts have been dominated by the pro-gun lobby, which has had a monopoly on influencing legislation and molding public opinion. The emergence of organized opposition to groups such as the NRA is a positive development that will foster a more balanced public dialogue on the subject. The intransigence of the gun lobby to such basic proposals as a national waiting period and the banning of assault rifles is a blatantly indefensible position, involving de minimus reforms which should not be considered the least bit controversial or threatening to law-abiding gun owners. It is certainly not too much to insist that greater scrutiny be exercised to keep firearms out of the hands of ineligible gun purchasers as well as individuals who are demonstrably violence-prone, mentally unstable, or socially irresponsible.

Making handguns inaccessible to all private citizens, save under narrowly defined conditions of "special need," is another matter. There is something incongruous about requiring the "good guys" to trade-off their defensive ownership of handguns because doing so might prevent a relatively small number of barroom altercations, domestic abuse incidents, or family quarrels from terminating in homicide—homicides which may be victim-precipitated or the result of victims making free choices to be in situations, places, or relationships fraught with danger. It is no secret that the current portrayal and reality of urban crime is dominated by accounts of "gun" violence and terrorism. There is a sense in which this anthropomorphism of firearms facilitates the displacement of culpability from the actual offender and diverts attention from the system's reluctance or inability to deal more effectively (before or after the fact) with this menacing gun-toting criminal element. Until such time as it does, it is unrealistic to expect or aspire to broadly based, unconditional disarmament of the general population.

# References

*A Question of Self-Defense* (1987). Washington, DC: NRA Institute for Legislative Action.

ABC News Closeup (1976). *Gun Control: Pro and Con* (April 20), transcript.

Alviani, J.D. & W.R. Drake (1984). *Handgun Control: Issues and Alternatives*. Chicago: U.S. Conference of Mayors.

Anderson, J. (1986). "Self-Defense is an Insufficient Argument Against Gun Control." In M.T. O'Neill & B. Szumski (eds.) *Opposing Viewpoints Sources: Criminal Justice 1986 Annual*, pp. 233-236. St. Paul, MN: Greenhaven Press.

Andrews, P. (1972). "A Day in a Gun Store." *Saturday Review*, (June 3): 15-16.

Ayoob, M.F. (1981). *The Police View of Gun Control*. Bellevue, WA: Second Amendment Foundation.

Baker, S.P., S.P. Teret & P.E. Dietz (1980). "Firearms and the Public Health." *Journal of Public Policy*, (September):224-229.

Beard, M.K. & K.M. Rand (1987). "The Handgun Battle." *Bill of Rights Journal*, (December):13-15.

Bendis, P. & S. Balkin (1979). "A Look at Gun Control Enforcement." *Journal of Police Science and Administration*, (December):439-448.

Benson, B.L. (1984). "Guns for Protection and Other Private Sector Responses to the Fear of Rising Crime." In D.B. Kates (ed.) *Firearms and Violence*, pp. 329-356. San Francisco: Pacific Institute for Public Policy Research.

Berkowitz, L. (1968). "Impulse, Aggression and the Gun." *Psychology Today*, (September):19-22.

_____ (1981). "How Guns Control Us." *Psychology Today*, (June):11-12.

Blackman, P.H. (1981). *Conceptual, Constitutional, Enforcement, and Experiential Problems Involved in Mandatory Sentencing for the Unlicensed Carrying/Possession of Handguns*. Washington, DC: NRA Institute for Legislative Action.

_____ (1985). "Gun Law Failure." *American Rifleman,* (August):34-35,78.

_____ (1988). *Firearms and Violence.* Washington, DC: NRA Institute for Legislative Action.

Bordua, D.J. (1984). "Adversary Polling and the Construction of Social Meaning." In D.B. Kates (ed.) *Firearms and Violence,* pp. 51-70. San Francisco: Pacific Institute for Public Policy Research.

Brill, S. (1977). *Firearms Abuse: A Research and Policy Report.* Washington, DC: Police Foundation.

Brown, T.P. (1986). "Ammunition for Victims of Saturday Night Specials: Manufacturer Liability Under *Kelly v. R.G. Industries." Washington and Lee Law Review,* (Fall):1315-1349.

Bruce-Briggs, B. (1976). "The Great American Gun War." *Public Interest,* (Fall):37-62.

Buchalter, G. (1988). "Why I Bought a Gun." *Parade Magazine,* (February 21):4ff.

Caplan, D.I. (1982). "The Right of the Individual to Bear Arms: A Recent Judicial Trend." *Detroit College of Law Review,* (Winter):789-823.

Center to Prevent Handgun Violence News Release (undated).

Clark, L.D. (1984). "Reducing Firearms Availability: Constitutional Impediments to Effective Legislation and an Agenda for Research." In D.B. Kates (ed.) *Firearms and Violence,* pp. 9-22. San Francisco: Pacific Institute for Public Policy Research.

Clotfelter, C.T. (1981). "Crimes, Disorders and the Demand for Handguns." *Law and Policy Quarterly,* (October):425-441.

Coleman, J. (1989). "Handgun Control" (private paper).

Cook, P. (1981a). "The Saturday Night Special: An Assessment of Alternative Definitions from a Policy Perspective." *Journal of Criminal Law and Criminology,* (Winter):1735-1745.

_____ (1981b). "The Effect of Gun Availability on Violent Crime Patterns." *Annals,* (May):63-79.

_____ (1983). "Influence of Gun Availability on Violent Crime Patterns." In M. Tonry & N. Morris (eds.) *Crime and Justice: An Annual Review of Research,* pp. 49-89. Chicago: University of Chicago Press.

Cook, P. & J. Blose (1981). "State Programs for Screening Handgun Buyers." *Annals,* (May):80-91.

*Crime Control Digest* (1975). (April 28):p.9.

Crime in the United States, 1987 (1988). *Uniform Crime Reports.* Washington, DC: Government Printing Office.

*Criminals Don't Wait: Why Should You* (1988). Washington, DC: NRA Institute for Legislative Action.

Danto, B. (1982). "Gun Control to Prevent Homicide and Suicide." In B. Danto, J. Bruhns & A.H. Kutscher (eds.) *The Human Side of Homicide,* pp. 209-221. New York: Columbia University Press.

Davies, P.S. (1986). "Saturday Night Specials: A Special Exception in Strict Liability Law." *Notre Dame Law Review,* 61:478-494.

Dole, R.J. (1986). "The Firearms Owners' Protection Act: A Defense." In M.T. O'Neill & B. Szumski (eds.) *Opposing Viewpoints Sources: Criminal Justice 1986 Annual,* pp. 221-222. St. Paul, MN: Greenhaven Press.

Drinan, R.F. (1976). "Gun Control: The Good Outweighs the Evil." *Civil Liberties Review,* (August/September):44-53.

Elias, C. (1987). "Handgun Industry Gets Fired Up." *Insight,* (November):40-43.

Freiburn, E.S. (1982). "Banning Handguns: *Quilici v. Village of Morton Grove* and the Second Amendment." *Washington University Law Quarterly,* 60:1087-1113.

Geisel, M.S., R. Roll & R.S. Wettick, Jr. (1969). "The Effectiveness of State and Local Regulation of Handguns: A Statistical Analysis." *Duke Law Journal,* (August):747-776.

Gettinger, S. (1980). "Police and Gun Control: Can the Law Reduce Bloodshed?" *Police Magazine,* (November):6-18.

Green, G.S. (1987). "Citizen Gun Ownership and Criminal Deterrence: Theory, Research and Policy." *Criminology,* (February):63-81.

Gun Control Press Release, July 10, 1988.

"Guns, Guns, Guns" (1988). NBC Summer Showcase, July 5, transcript.

Halbrook, S.P. (1983). "Tort Liability for the Manufacture, Sale and Ownership of Handguns." *Hamline Law Review,* (July):351-382.

Handgun Violence Protection Act of 1987. Testimony before the Subcommittee on the Constitution of the Senate Judiciary.

"Handguns and Product Liability." (1984). *Harvard Law Review,* (June): 1912-1928.

Hardy, D.T. (1987). "Product Liability and Weapons Manufacture." *Journal of Products Liability,* 10:61-90.

Harris, R. (1976). "Handguns." *New Yorker,* (July 26):53ff.

Jacobs, J.B. (1986). "Exceptions to a General Prohibition on Handgun Possession: Do they Swallow up the Rule?" *Law and Contemporary Problems,* (Winter):5-34.

*Justice Reporter* (1981) "Handgun Control: Three Views." (Fall):1-8.

Kaplan, J. (1979). "Controlling Firearms." *Cleveland State Law Review,* 28:1-28.

———— (1981). "The Wisdom of Gun Prohibition." *Annals,* (May):11-23.

———— (1984). "Foreword" to D.B. Kates (ed.) *Firearms and Violence,* pp. xxiii-xxxi. San Francisco: Pacific Institute for Public Policy Research.

———— (1986). Foreword to *Law and Contemporary Problems,* 49(Winter):1-3.

Kates, D.B. (1976a). "Why a Civil Libertarian Opposes Gun Control." *Civil Liberties Review,* (June/July):24-32.

———— (1976b). "Rejoinder." *Civil Liberties Review,* (August/September):53-59.

———— (ed.) (1979). *Restricting Handguns: The Liberal Skeptics Speak Out.* Croton-on-Hudson, NY: North River Press.

———— (1983). "Handgun Prohibition and the Original Meaning of the Second Amendment." *Michigan Law Review,* 82(November):204-273.

———— (1984). "Handgun Banning in Light of the Prohibition Experience." In D.B. Kates (ed.) *Firearms and Violence,* pp. 139-165. San Francisco: Pacific Institute for Public Policy Research.

———— (1986a). "The Battle Over Gun Control." *Public Interest,* (Summer):42-52.

———— (1986b). "The Second Amendment: A Dialogue." *Law and Contemporary Problems,* (Winter):143-149.

Kellerman, A.L. & D.T. Reay (1986). "Protection or Peril: An Analysis of Firearms-Related Deaths in the Home." *New England Journal of Medicine,* (June):1557-1560.

Kessler, R.G. (1980). "Enforcement Problems of Gun Control: A Victimless Crime Analysis." *Criminal Law Bulletin* (March/April):131-149.

Kleck, G. (1984a). "The Assumptions of Gun Control." In D.B. Kates (ed.) *Firearms and Violence,* pp. 23-44. San Francisco: Pacific Institute for Public Policy Research.

_____ (1984b). "The Relationship Between Gun Ownership Levels and Rates of Violence in the United States." In D.B. Kates (ed.) *Firearms and Violence*, pp. 99-132. San Francisco: Pacific Institute for Public Policy Research.

_____ (1984c). "Handgun-Only Gun Control: A Policy Disaster in the Making." In D.B. Kates (ed.) *Firearms and Violence*, pp. 167-199. San Francisco: Pacific Institute for Public Policy Research.

_____ (1986a). "Saturday Night Special Not Very Important for Crime." *Sociology and Social Research*, 70(July):303-307.

_____ (1986b). "Policy Lessons from Recent Gun Control Research." *Law and Contemporary Problems*, (Winter):35-62.

_____ (1988). "Crime Control through the Private Use of Armed Force." *Social Problems*, (February):1-21.

Kleck, G., D.B. Kates, D. Bordua, J. Magaddino & M.H. Medoff (1982). *Why Handgun Bans Can't Work*. Bellevue, WA: Second Amendment Foundation.

Kluin, K.F. (1982). "Gun Control: Is it a Legal and Effective Means for Controlling Firearms?" *Washington Law Journal*, 21(2):244-265.

Lapp, D.J. (1987). "The Application of Strict Liability to Manufacturers and Sellers of Handguns: A Call for More Focused Debate." *Journal of Products Liability*, 10:179-196. *Law Enforcement News*, (1989), (January 31):6ff.

Lester, D. (1984). *Gun Control: Issues and Answers*. Springfield, IL: Charles C Thomas.

Lester, D. & M.E. Murrell (1982). "Preventive Effect of Strict Gun Control Laws on Suicide and Homicide." *Suicide and Life-Threatening Behavior*, 12(Fall):131-140.

Magaddino, J.P. & M.H. Medoff (1984). "An Empirical Analysis of Federal and State Firearm Control Laws." In D.B. Kates (ed.) *Firearms and Violence*, pp. 225-258. San Francisco: Pacific Institute for Public Policy Research.

Marina, W. (1984). "Weapons, Technology, and Legitimacy: The Second Amendment in Global Perspective." In D.B. Kates (ed.) *Firearms and Violence*, pp. 417-418. San Francisco: Pacific Institute for Public Policy Research.

McClain, P.D. (1984). "Prohibiting the SNS: A Feasible Policy Option?" In D.B. Kates (ed.) *Firearms and Violence*, pp. 201-217. San Francisco: Pacific Institute for Public Policy Research.

McDermott, J.M. (1979). *Rape Victimization in 26 American Cities.* Washington, DC: Government Printing Office.

Moore, M.H. (1981). "Keeping Handguns from Criminal Offenders." *Annals,* (May):92-109.

Murray, D.R. (1975). "Handguns, Gun Control Laws and Firearm Violence." *Social Problems,* (October):81-92.

National Coalition to Ban Handguns. Saturday Night Special Fact Sheet.

National Institute of Justice Crime File, Study Guide on Gun Control.

*National Law Journal* (1989a). "How Lawyers Helped One City Ban Rifles." (March 6):3ff.

―――― (1989b). "Guns Out of Control." (April 13):57. *New Republic* (1988). "Go Ahead, Make Our Day" (February 22):7-9.

*Newsweek* (1981). "Guns Out of Control." (April 13):57.

―――― (1982). "A New Push for Gun Control." (March 15):22-23.

―――― (1988a). "Looking for the Good Guys." (February 15):10.

―――― (1988b). "New Support for Gun Control." (August 15):26.

―――― (1989a). "Death on the Playground." (January 30):35.

―――― (1989b) "The NRA Comes Under the Gun." (March 27):28ff.

―――― (1989c). "I Told Them I'd Be Back." (September 25):22.

Newton, G.D. & F.E. Zimring (1968). *Firearms and Violence in American Life: A Staff Report to the National Commission on the Causes and Prevention of Violence.* Washington, DC: Superintendent of Documents.

*New York Times* (1975a). "It's Easy to Get Guns that Find Way to Northeast." (March 13):24.

―――― (1975b). "U.S.-Made Pistols are Said to Break Import Law." (April 13):53.

―――― (1981). "Rifle Group Viewed as Key to Gun Law." (April 5):31.

―――― (1985a). "How to Deter Future Hinckleys." (November 8):A35.

―――― (1985b). "Half of States Use Only U.S. Gun Curb." (November 24):40.

―――― (1986a). "Measure to Relax Gun Rules Denounced by Police Groups." (January 31):A16.

―――― (1986b). "Will Handgun Foes be over a Barrel?" (March 28):A35.

_____ (1986c). "House Passes Bill Easing Controls on Sale of Guns."(April 11):1,D18.

_____ (1986d). "Charged Under a Ban on Pistols." (October 26):32.

_____ (1987a). "Georgia Town to Celebrate Mandatory Firearms." (April 11):10.

_____ (1987b). "A Way to Control Handguns." (April 15):A27.

_____ (1987c). "Guns in Florida." (September 27):26.

_____ (1987d). "Florida Closes Dodge City Loophole." (October 25):E5.

_____ (1988a). "Floridians Find it Easy to Get Permits to Carry Hidden Guns." (March 9):A24.

_____ (1988b). "New Law in Maryland Bans Sale and Manufacture of Some Pistols." (May 24):D27.

_____ (1988c). "Foes Dig In on Gun Ban in Md." (June 5):22.

_____ (1988d). "Gun Control Backers Say Maryland Victory Will Spread to Other States." (November 13):30.

_____ (1989a). "After Shooting, Horror But Few Answers." (January 19):B6.

_____ (1989b). "Effort to Ban Assault Rifles Gains Momentum." (January 28):1ff.

_____ (1989c). "Impact of Curbs on Guns Debated." (March 16):11.

_____ (1989d). "U.S. Widens Import Curbs on Military-Like Rifles."(April 6):A24.

_____ (1991). "Gun Control Bill Backed by Reagan in Appeal to Bush." (March 29):1.

*One Million Strong.* Handgun Control Inc.

Pierce, G.L. & W.J. Bowers (1981). "The Bartley-Fox Law's Short-Term Impact on Crime in Boston." *Annals,* (May):120-137.

Public Law 99-308, May 19, 1986, 99th Congress, 100 Stat. 449-461, effective November 15, 1986.

Rand, M., M. DeBerry, P. Klaus & B. Taylor (1986). *The Use of Weapons in Committing Crimes.* Washington, DC: Bureau of Justice Special Report.

*Report to the Nation on Crime and Justice* (1988). Washington, DC: Bureau of Justice Statistics.

Riley, R.J. (1974). "Shooting to Kill the Handgun: Time to Martyr Another American Hero." *Journal of Urban Law,* 51 (February):491-524.

Rose, H.M. & D.R. Deskins (1986) "Handguns and Homicide in Black Communities." In D.F. Hawkins (ed.) *Homicide Among Black Americans,* pp. 69-100. Lanham, MD: University Press of America.

Rossman, D., P. Froyd, G.L. Pierce, J. McDevitt & W.J. Bowers (1980). "Massachusetts' Mandatory Minimum Sentence Gun Law: Enforcement, Prosecution, and Defense Impact." *Criminal Law Bulletin,* (March-April):150-163.

Rushforth, N.B., C.S. Hirsch, A.A. Ford & L. Adelson (1975). "Accidental Firearm Fatalities in a Metropolitan County." *American Journal of Epidemiology,* 100:499-505.

*Sample Firearms Regulations in Illinois Municipalities* (1983). Chicago: Illinois Citizens for Handgun Control.

Sherman, L.W. (1980). "The Police and the Mandatory Gun Law." *Criminal Law Bulletin,* (March-April):164-167.

Shields, P. (1981). *Guns Don't Die—People Do.* New York City: Arbor House Publishing Co.

Spitzer, R.J. (1986). "Gun Control is Not a Violation of Constitutional Rights." In M.T. O'Neill & B. Szumski (eds.) *Opposing Viewpoints Sources: Criminal Justice 1986 Annual,* pp. 243-244. St. Paul, MN: Greenhaven Press.

Steffy, M.S. (1986). "Manufacturers' or Marketers' Liability for the Criminal Use of Saturday Night Specials: A New Common Law Approach." *Florida State University Law Review,* (Spring):149-165.

*Ten Myths About Gun Control* (1987). National Rifle Association Institute for Legislative Action.

*The Banner* (1987). National Coalition to Ban Handguns, 3(2):1-4.

*Time* (1981). "Magnum-Force Lobby." (April 20):22

———— (1987a). "Pistol Packers." (September 28):28.

———— (1987b). "Goodbye Gunshine." (October 19):25.

———— (1988a). "Maryland's $10,000 Per Handgun." (April 25):45.

———— (1988b). "Why Wait a Week to Kill?" (September 26):26.

———— (1988c). "The NRA Targets a Tough Law." (November 7, 1988):36.

———— (1989a). "Armed America." (February 6):20ff.

———— (1989b). "Have Weapons, Will Shoot." (February 27):22.

———— (1989c). "Gunning for Assault Rifles." (March 27):39.

———— (1989d). "The NRA in a Hunter's Sights." (April 3):86.

Turley, W. (1982). "Manufacturers' and Suppliers' Liability to Handgun Victims." *Northern Kentucky Law Review*, 10:41-62.

*USA Today* (1985). "Gun Town Piece has City up in Arms." (November 29):3A.

———— (1987a). "Delaying Gun Sales Will Stop Criminals," (May 26):12A.

———— (1987b). "Critics, Police Fear Calamity and Carnage of New Florida Gun Law." (October 1):1A-2A.

———— (1987c). "Florida's Gunsmoke Law Takes Effect." (October 2):3A.

———— (1987d). (October 19):3A.

———— (1988a). "Police Shooting Revives Florida Gun Control Battle." (April 29):3A.

———— (1988b). "Md. Gun Ban Foes Aim at Nov. Repeal." (June 13):3A.

———— (1988c). "Owing Gun No Right." (August 8):3A.

———— (1988d). "Make Buyers Wait." (August 9):10A.

———— (1988e). (November 17):3A.

———— (1988f). "Stiff Fines Backbone of Md. Law." (May 24):1A.

———— (1988g). "Gun Shop Settles in Miami Shooting." (July 15):3A.

———— (1989). (September 15):9A.

———— (1991). "Reagan Gives Brady Bill Backers a Boost." (March 29):1.

*U.S. News & World Report* (1980) "Should Handguns be Outlawed?" (December 22):23-24.

———— (1986a). "High Noon on Gun Control." (March 17):74.

———— (1986b). "Congress in a Cross Fire in Battle over Gun Control." (March 24):20.

———— (1987a). "Dissidents, Old Allies Shake NRA." (April 27):44.

———— (1987b). "Local Gun Controls Bite the Dust." (May 25):14-15.

———— (1987c). "Florida's New Crop of Pistol Packers." (October 12):16.

———— (1988a). "Congress Makes NRA's Day." (April 21):8.

———— (1988b). "The NRA Nails a New Coonskin to the Wall." (September 26):11.

_____ (1989a). "The Next Wave of Gun Control." (February 27):30.

_____ (1989b). "Lock and Load for the Gunfight." (March 27):9.

Wagner, Bill (1988). "Strict Liability: A Doctrine Providing a Solution." *National Law Journal*, (August):15ff.

*Washington Report* (1988). 14(Spring):1.

*What You Should Know About the Brady Bill*. Handgun Control Inc. (undated).

Wintemute, G., S.P. Teret, J.F. Kraus & M.W. Wright (1988). "The Choice of Weapon in Firearms Suicides." *American Journal of Public Health*, (July):824-826.

Wolfgang, M.E. (1958). *Patterns in Criminal Homicide*. Philadelphia: University of Pennsylvania.

Wright, J.D. (1981). "Public Opinion and Gun Control: A Comparison of Results from Two Recent National Surveys." *Annals*, (May):245-239.

_____ (1984). "The Ownership of Firearms for Reasons of Self Defense." In D.B. Kates (ed.) *Firearms and Violence*, pp. 301-327. San Francisco: Pacific Institute for Public Policy Research.

_____ (1986). *The Armed Criminal in America*. Washington, DC: National Institute of Justice.

_____ (1988). "Second Thoughts about Gun Control." *Public Interest*, 91(Spring):23-39.

_____ & L.L. Marston (1975). "The Ownership of the Means of Destruction: Weapons in the United States." *Social Problems*, (October):93-107.

_____ & P.H. Rossi (1986). *Armed and Considered Dangerous: A Survey of Felons and their Firearms*. New York: Aldine De Gruyter.

_____ P.H. Rossi & K. Daly (1983). *Under the Gun: Weapons, Crime and Violence in America*. New York: Aldine Publishing Co.

Wright, J.D., P.H. Rossi, K. Daly & E. Weber-Burdin (1981). *Weapons, Crime and Violence in America: A Literature Review and Agenda*. Washington, DC: Government Printing Office.

Young, R.L., D. McDowall & C. Loftin (1987). "Collective Security and the Ownership of Firearms for Protection." *Criminology*, (February):47-62.

Zimring, F.E. (1968). "Is Gun Control Likely to Reduce Violent Killings?" *University of Chicago Law Review*, (Summer):721-737.

_____ (1975). "Firearms and Federal Law: The Gun Control Act of 1968." *Journal of Legal Studies*, (January):133-198.